A Place of Your Own

To Mona and Tony,
warm regards
Edward Amul
Dec. 1998

A Place of Your Own

Edward Searl

BERKLEY BOOKS, NEW YORK

This book is an original publication of The Berkley Publishing Group.

A PLACE OF YOUR OWN

A Berkley Book / published by arrangement with
the author

PRINTING HISTORY
Berkley trade paperback edition / December 1998

The Penguin Putnam Inc. World Wide Web site address is
http://www.penguinputnam.com

ISBN: 0-425-16546-9

BERKLEY®
Berkley Books are published by The Berkley Publishing Group, a member of
Penguin Putnam Inc., 375 Hudson Street, New York, New York 10014.
BERKLEY and the "B" design are trademarks belonging to Berkley Publishing
Corporation.

PRINTED IN THE UNITED STATES OF AMERICA

10   9   8   7   6   5   4   3   2   1

*To Ellie Volckmann Searl, loving and loyal companion,
sturdy support, and uncanny guide during the first thirty years
of our Great Adventure*

acknowledgments

Much of the material of this book, in creation and inspiration, relates to hundreds of persons I've known and loved in my congregations in Youngstown, Ohio, and Hinsdale, Illinois. They gave me the rare privilege of trying out my writings on a relational audience—both receptive and critical. Through them, I found my voice as well as my vocation.

I thank my literary agent Sheree Bykofsky, who recognized the possibilities of this book. Her enthusiasm transformed an idea into a viable commercial project. I am particularly grateful for the skill and respect of my editor, Lisa Considine, who guided my sometimes vague intentions into a focused and more coherent design. Both women were incredibly accessible and responsive throughout a quickly unfolding process.

contents

S U M M E R

Contents

introduction

A Place of Your Own explores something you already do, but probably don't think much about, if you think about it at all: claiming space in your home for significant, meaningful objects. In doing this you make what are natural, personal altars for essentially spiritual purposes: creativity, beauty, memory, and connection. Your natural altar may be as ordinary as a collection of family photographs on top of a dresser, a handful of souvenir seashells laid on a windowsill, or inspirational sayings attached by magnets to the side of the refrigerator. These areas and their like are sacred spaces—places you've claimed and imbued with meaning through tangible things and intangible intentions. These are places of ownership and belonging, from which you take solace and insight.

A few years ago I realized, with some surprise, that my life and home were full of such places. I decided to construct a piece of furniture to be my home altar and explore ways to enhance my private spiritual life. I found the process and practice incredibly rewarding. Not only did my home altar influence my spirituality, it brought much beauty and many blessings into my home.

This book will help you discover and develop your natural instinct to create altars. It describes what led me to create a home altar and my experiments with its use. It offers practical suggestions about how to build upon your instincts and create your own home altar. I'll suggest objects you might want to collect—objects to use in conjunction with your altar in celebrating holidays, seasons, and occasions. Or perhaps meditation and worship are your goals. In either case, I've also provided fifty-two thematic devotions to harmonize you with the rhythms of a typical year. I hope they will encourage you to develop your own collection of meaningful readings.

No less an authority than Jesus taught that true spirituality is a private matter. In the Sermon on the Mount, as told by the apostle Matthew, he taught his followers not to be like the hypocrites who make a display of prayer in synagogues and on street corners. He said, "When you pray, go into your room and shut the door and pray . . . in secret. . . . [D]o not heap up empty phrases." (RSV, Matt. 6:6–8)

Contemporary scholars of the "new historical quest for Jesus" have recognized that Jesus emphasized direct relationships. In other words, no one else should broker or mediate your relationships, with others or with the Divine. The Buddha likewise taught that enlightenment wasn't something that could be negotiated, but rather was a matter of direct, personal experience. A home altar encourages private, heartfelt devotion and intimate, direct relationships—the sort of spirituality that can only be realized in a place of your own where you invite and invoke the transcendent.

You can bring your faith tradition to your home altar. Mexican homes have traditionally had home altars, not formally recognized but tacitly accepted by Catholic clergy for centuries. Many Mexican Americans continue this tradition in the United States. In the late nineteenth century, Protestants used the phrase *home altar* to describe a regular and orderly practice of family devotional readings. Jewish traditions, Hanukkah and Passover for example, encourage home celebrations and family ritual. Eastern traditions—Hinduism, Buddhism, Taoism, Confucianism—incorporate home shrines dedicated to particular gods or the Buddha spirit.

A home altar suits a range of practices from casual to complex. Those practices can be independent of your faith tradition or they can supplement and enrich it.

A home altar is readily accessible and remarkably adaptable. It is intimate and private, yet it connects you to larger rhythms and transcendent inspirations. I don't know any other spiritual discipline more natural and common. Despite our culture, which yearns for and continuously seeks spirituality, it's not a discipline that is well known or much practiced. But you need only to acknowledge your natural instinct to create sacred places in order to begin to appreciate how a home altar might satisfy much of your spiritual yearning. Building on this instinct will give you a place of your own that is a spiritual home.

A Place of My Own

O nce in a while I get the urge to make something out of wood. A few years ago I built a meditation fountain—a low cedar box in a Japanese style, thirty inches long and twenty inches wide, with a plastic liner, and a circulating pump. I framed the open top with five-inch cedar boards and lifted it from the floor on short legs. The completed fountain seemed just right. It had attractive proportions and was made from materials I was naturally drawn to. The water washed over a large rock I picked up in the muddy Rio Grande at its Big Bend in Texas and around smaller cobblestones from an icy Adirondack Mountains stream.

I placed the fountain in my living room and enjoyed the pleasant, gurgling sound of flowing water. It brought nature into my home through wood, rocks, and water.

As soon as I set up my meditation fountain, I felt compelled to arrange objects on the fountain's broad frame. Wherever I go I collect stones, so I selected a few from my cache: several small, flat stones with round holes cut through them gathered from Lake

Michigan and Lake Superior beaches, a fist-sized yellow and brown agate from Montana's Yellowstone River, a polished piece of yellow and red poppy seed jasper from Northern California, a crumbly piece of gray montmorillonite from a friend's mine in Chimayo, New Mexico. Each rock held a special memory. I bought a small Asian fern and a terra-cotta pot to place among the rocks. I wanted candlelight and settled upon a votive candle in a simple cobalt blue. I returned from a bike ride with long splinters a lightning strike had torn from an old elm tree. As a tribute to nature's power, I arranged those splinters in a blue Van Briggle vase, a treasure I'd found in a Chicago thrift store.

Friends who saw my fountain and the objects arranged on the frame spontaneously gave me more things to add to my collection. One friend gave me a pot she'd hand-turned for my fern. Another gave me a realistic wood carving of three toad-stools. Several friends, knowing my fondness for rocks, gave me stones they'd collected on their travels. I added these gifts to the fountain's frame.

On impulse, I bought an expensive horizontal oil painting. The narrow panel portrayed a series of Japanese objects and a chalk-faced, doll-like geisha. I loved its haunting icon-like images and when I got home I realized I'd bought it to place on my fountain as a backdrop to accent the Japanese style.

With these objects arranged on it, my fountain had become a visual focus in addition to being the source of pleasant gurgling. It had become something unexpected. Ever changing, it seemed to have a life of its own. I understood what I was creating was an expression of me. *Its* life related to *my* life, because it was home to things that were meaningful to me.

The urge to arrange special objects on my fountain intrigued me. The evolving arrangements and the satisfaction I found in them fascinated me. Why did the arrangements give me so much satisfaction? Why did they hold my attention for stretches of quiet contemplation?

One day I realized what I'd created: My fountain was an altar! I was amazed. I didn't see myself as the sort of person for whom a home altar had meaning. I was even a little uncomfortable using the word "altar"; but that's exactly what I'd fashioned. My eyes had been opened. My mind delighted in the insights from this revelation. I had expanded my own sense of spiritual practice.

An altar is a designated place—often an elevated structure or area—of spiritual focus and ritual activity. It is sacred space that in religious language is *numinous*—charged with the transcendent spirit of the Divine. That spirit is inherent in the altar area and is also a function of what a person brings to their special place through tangible objects and intangible intentions. Through an altar, including the objects placed on it and the acts performed around it, a person invokes and has a relationship with the transcendent. It's a place to invite, to talk to, and to know God. It's a place of aspiration of and dedication to ideals. It's a place to bring and grow your soul.

In the instant I realized I'd created an altar, I also realized it was something I'd been doing throughout my life. Indeed, I was *just* the sort of person for whom a home altar had meaning.

My mind flashed images of many altars I had fashioned in the places I had lived.

I counted two altars in my office: a long windowsill behind my desk and a pine bookcase in a dark corner. Most of the objects on my office altars were gifts. My windowsill displayed a miniature Zen sand garden with a tiny rake and rocks; a handful of polished amethyst, tigereye, quartz, and hematite stones; a goofy pottery bird; an antique ink blotter; an elephant ashtray carved from water buffalo horn brought back from Vietnam by my Vietnamese janitor; and a tiny pewter prospector perched on a piece of fool's gold that a former secretary brought back from Las Vegas. The bookcase held agate bookends; a roly-poly golden plastic Buddha that laughed when tipped; cocktail glasses from a Cajun bar; a broken dish lovingly reassembled and displayed on its own stand; and a 150-year-old framed autograph of the famous Unitarian minister Theodore Parker. Each of these objects had its own story, each recalled a personal relationship. My office altars reminded me of and connected me with many friends from the congregation I'd served for fifteen years.

I'd also appointed two areas in my home as altars. A small built-in bookcase to one side of the living-room fireplace held several valuable pieces of art glass, which friends had given me in appreciation for weddings I'd performed or counseling I'd done when I'd refused honoraria. I added contemporary and antique pottery vases I'd collected through the years. Each piece of pottery represented special places and times of my life. Among the art glass and pottery I'd placed smaller objects: a wood carving of a man in a rocking chair, from Quebec where I once lived; seashells gathered from several vacation beaches; a brown jasper buffalo given to me by my music director; a terra-cotta figure of a winsome woman holding a rose, which I had bought in New Mexico during a Holy Week pilgrimage; a small string art painting by a Yacqui shaman; a stained-glass souvenir from an Arts and Crafts show at Chicago's Art Institute. Each of these objects had a particular association—a treasured time, place, or relationship.

The top of an old upright piano on an opposite wall was another sort of altar. There were photographs of my small family. My profile, taken in Calgary fifteen years ago on an auspicious June morning, commanded a corner. My daughter's face smiles from her high school graduation portrait. My wife and I, arm in arm, look out of a twenty-year-old snapshot. Included in this grouping was a child's drawing on notebook paper of a little girl with her arms outstretched and an irregular block letter epithet—I LOVE EVERYBODY IN THE WORLD SPESBLY YOU—drawn for us by our daughter Katy, some twenty years ago. These objects, which convey a sense of the passage and richness of time, never fail to fill me with poignant emotion.

My office and home altars each relate to their particular setting. The altars in my office bring the focus of personal relationships into the room where I write my sermons, counsel, and administrate the church I serve. These two office altars humanize the shelves of books and notebooks filled with old sermons, the gray metal file cabinets, the worn furniture, and the desk cluttered with a computer and piles of papers. They remind me that my first commitment is to real people and not to ideas or institutions. The altars in my home are more artistic arrangements, which beautify my home. They make my home more home-like, through their representations and reminders of the family who make this place their home, the lives they live, and the things they love.

Altars Everywhere

When I recognized that my meditation fountain had evolved into a recognizable altar and that I had, in fact, made many altars, I decided to explore and build upon my instinct to make them. I planned a special altar for my home. I sketched a design and considered the materials I'd use. I also mused on the influences and inspirations that converged in my new passion. The project seemed more than timely. It was inevitable. It was a new passage in my pilgrim's progress, a conjunction of twenty-five years of spiritual inquiry, which began with theological study at McGill University and continued for twenty years of practical work as a Unitarian minister.

The free and eclectic liberal religious tradition I embraced gave me my vocation. It also provided encouragement and opportunity to pursue my avocation, what I call *Natural Religion*— the living religion of the human condition and spirit. I drew my best understandings and insights from psychology, poetry, literature, art, architecture, and, most of all, firsthand experience. I firmly believe that religion is natural to the human condition. I also believe the greatest religious teachers, Buddha and Jesus, for example, sought to set human beings free as individuals to directly experience the transcendent—the Divine Spirit or God.

An intuition persuaded me that an intentional altar would help me in my ongoing search for direct experience of the Divine. That intuition rested in converging influences and inspirations I'd acquired gradually over the span of a quarter of a century. The chronological order of these influences and inspirations echoed my spiritual journey. They converged in a genuine passion—I decided to construct a piece of furniture with which I could explore and nuture my instinct to make altars.

An early inspiration was Carl Jung, whose work I first read in a Psychology of Religion course at McGill. His autobiography impressed me, particularly the account of a private retreat he built on the shore of Lake Geneva. It began as a tower he constructed with his own hands from native materials. He called his creation a "confession of faith in stone." Over the years, in response to his own inner urgings and psychic growth, he added to it. The heart of it all, at the top of the tower, was a private retiring room. Jung kept his tower locked. Visitors entered only with his permission. He painted his visions as frescoes on its walls. In this intimate and sacred space, he acted out, in a most symbolic setting, his inner spirituality.

I had long wanted just such a retiring place, but realized I would never have Jung's resources. A relatively modest altar would serve similar purposes: a place to create and commune, an outer expression of my inner being and spiritual aspirations.

The first church I served was a remnant congregation struggling to survive, the First Unitarian Church of Youngstown,

Ohio. The church owned a handsome building—a 1920s red brick and white wood replica of an old Boston church. It had a traditional raised pulpit, large chancel area, and a seven-foot-long altar. Circumstances gave me free reign. The altar begged for attention. In the first few months, I stripped the dark varnish, which had dulled over the years, and restored a red mahogany luster that glowed. I enjoyed creating great arrangements on it and bought oversized vases, candlesticks, and handwoven runners. It is said that the tradition of flowers in Protestant churches began with Unitarian churches of Boston in the mid-1800s. I built on that tradition with great vases of goldenrod and cattails in autumn, boughs of evergreens and holly in winter, and tiers of small azaleas in spring. I borrowed large works of art—paintings, quilts, and banners—to hang on the wall behind the altar. My experiences in Youngstown satisfied some of my yearning for a place of my own. They also awakened my delight in creating altar arrangements.

I missed that hands-on creativity in my next, and current, church in Hinsdale, Illinois, a Chicago suburb. In Hinsdale the flowers are provided by a member who is a florist. The flowers are displayed on a tall pedestal, which stands to one side of a raised platform filled by a portable oak pulpit and a gleaming grand piano. That there isn't an altar reflects the congregation's long-standing humanist outlook.

The Hinsdale church building, an Arts and Crafts chapel erected in 1886, profoundly shaped my spirituality. Its first minister, William Channing Gannett, incorporated in the building's design elements his celebrated essay "House Beautiful." That essay, through the efforts of Gannett's intimate friend, Frank Lloyd Wright, became an inspiration for the popular magazine of the same name. In the essay Gannett described the fundamental relationship between the domestic and the Divine and recommended simple attitudes, acts, and arrangements to bring the Divine into everyday life. What Gannett called "domestication of the infinite" was such an important concept that he designed the Hinsdale building as a church *home*. The simple, handwrought Arts and Crafts–style of the era perfectly suited Gannett's purposes. In the main area, a living room opens into an auditorium. A fireplace, its hearth a symbol of the family, graces each room.

The unpretentious, humanly scaled, and domestic features of the Hinsdale church infused me with a practical understanding of and appreciation for making the home a sacred place. Gannett's intentions and design convinced me that the simple values of a home—family, comfort, beauty, good books, conversation, love, and friends—are the wellsprings of society's values and culture. Religion, too, has its continuing source in the domestic or ordinary life of human beings. Its first expressions are the family and the home.

For fifteen years I made an annual event of going to see the Day of the Dead (*Dia de los Muertos*) displays in Chicago's Mexican Museum of Fine Arts. The altars (*ofrendas*) and other traditional Mexican folk art honor the dead at the Christian festivals of All Saints and All Souls days on November 1 and 2. Public altars are outgrowths of a long-standing Mexican tradition of home altars. At first sight the fantastic public altars

seemed more kitsch than art, more parody than reverent remembrance. Still they intrigued me. I came to appreciate how
they honored the deceased. I studied the symbols: yellow chrysanthemums, sugar skulls and coffins, cut paper streamers of
skeletons, offerings of objects and foods. I learned of the pre-
Christian traditions that melded with the church's All Saints
and All Souls days. Drawing from my years of experience in grief
counseling and study of comparative religions, I acknowledged
that the yearly ritual of creating altars to honor the dead is a
psychologically sound, as well as spiritually rich, way of dealing
with death. Though death is a solemn and fearful subject, the
Day of the Dead has much playfulness, which encourages us to
confront mortality and, through that, to honor life.

I envied the psychic freedom the Day of the Dead altars
allowed. I sensed that just creating them—choosing and arranging objects to signify and symbolize a loved one—was a
spiritual act. These altars had the same sort of spiritual richness
I imagined in Jung's tower retreat. Their playfulness seemed an
antidote to the deadly seriousness and lack of imagination I'd
acquired from my culture and had long sought to overcome.

Four years earlier, in a small adobe sanctuary in Chimayo,
New Mexico, while on an epic sabbatical road trip, I encountered centuries-old wooden panels that portrayed the lives of
locally significant saints. They'd been painted to communicate
spiritual truths to illiterate parishioners. Though I couldn't in-
terpret the specific symbolisms and references of the complex
paintings without a guidebook, the panels held my attention. I
sat for a long time in the dimly lit, aromatic sanctuary and stud-

ied them. A power flowed from the primitive, earnest art to my religious consciousness.

I'd spent a lifetime using words and had come to a juncture where words and the abstract ideas they conveyed had topped out. I was being drawn to the nonverbal and concrete, because they promised to take my spiritual quest beyond the limits of words and abstractions to greater understanding.

Later that year, browsing in a Chinese furniture store in Los Angeles, I first saw what I have since learned is a common form of Buddhist altar. It's a substantial cabinet—chest high, with doors and sliding shelves that open to become an altar on which a statue of the Buddha, or a household god, might be placed along with sticks of incense and other offerings. The design struck me as cunning and practical—a versatile piece of furniture, which helped keep the altar private and out of visitors' sights, yet was ready in a moment. Buying the cabinet and shipping it to Chicago was beyond my means. Anyway, the Chinese design didn't feel like my style.

In recent years, I have become a frequent visitor of a small neighborhood gallery of Chicago artist Marya Veeck. Replete with icon-like images, some of traditional religious imagery, her paintings were arranged on what I saw to be tiered altars. They were outpourings of her unconscious, but beyond that they spoke of spiritual connection. After we became friends, Marya invited me into her rooms above the gallery to show me her most private work: a miniature roofless house of rooms that she arranged and rearranged. "A doll house," her friends joked. But they couldn't have been more wrong. The rooms contained in the house represented the beloved dead of her life. Marya explained that a front room with a black and white tiled floor and bed represented her father. I'd seen that black and white tiled floor in her larger paintings. It was clear to me that the process of creating art gave her spiritual therapy rich in private understandings.

Subsequently I saw that her private rooms and studio housed many altars and shrines: a small Mexican tin cabinet with a variety of small objects on its shelves; a shelf with photographs and other objects memorializing a deceased brother; more roofless miniature houses; and, by her easel, a wall and tabletop full of priceless baseball memorabilia, dedicated to her larger-than-life father Bill Veeck.

I was ready to adopt a new vernacular—wordless and tangible—to communicate from and with a deeper self. Marya Veeck's art encouraged and enthused me. The discovery of Marya's altars marked the beginning of my passion to make an altar as a place of my own. I had an artist's soul yearning to create.

By My Own Hand

A design for my altar appeared in my imagination, all at once, a nearly complete vision—a matter of inspiration and intuition. I envisioned a relatively tall, graceful piece of occasional furniture topped by a hinged shallow box. When lifted, the lid would unfold and open like a triptych to define the altar and reveal a rectangle of glazed tiles that defined the altar surface. The inside of the lid and the two hinged sides, when opened, might display small paintings and photographs. With the lid left down the whole piece would be a graceful, rather tall piece of furniture—a cross between an end table and a fern stand executed in a vaguely Art Deco style—suitable for a large vase of flowers or a flowing plant.

I sketched it on paper to work out the practical considerations of fashioning the legs and attaching them to the body. I worked up dimensions that corresponded to materials I might use. I prowled a local builder supply for wood. My choices recalled special times and places. Red cedar paid homage to the kitschy, rustic souvenirs of my boyhood. I considered leaving the inside of the lid unfinished so the aroma of the cedar would scent the room. The knotted white pine reminded me of my six-year sojourn in Quebec, where the most desirable antiques are white pine, turned a honey hue by age and use. I'd purchased the hand-painted Mexican tile in Albuquerque a few years earlier.

I started the project by fashioning the shallow lid and hinged panels from thin, red cedar boards. I arrived at the dimensions by trial and error. I cut and glued a top and added sides with glue and brass brads to shape the lid. I hung two side panels with brass hinges on the inside of the lid. This lid was the most problematic piece. After I found its proportions and built it, the rest of the altar fell into place. Next I cut a frame, fourteen by twenty-six inches, for the top and set its center with glazed squares of yellow, red, and blue tile. Then I experimented with long legs—forty-five inches long and tapered to give an illusion of lightness—cut from heavily knotted, five-inch-wide pine planks set at the corners. The result came close to what I'd seen in my imagination. Leaving the cedar and pine their natural color, I applied several coats of satin finish varnish.

I took a couple of months to make my altar. I wasn't in a hurry, and I solved construction problems as I progressed. Each step along the way gave me a sense of accomplishment. It was certainly my creation into which I poured my mind and spirit. It had the imprint of my hands. I didn't take pains to make it flawless. I actually preferred the imperfections of materials and craftsmanship—signatures of the moment of creation that the Japanese cherish and name *wabi*.

Lid down, my altar was in repose. Lid up and side panels open, it was a functional altar. I placed it to one side of the fireplace in the living area of my house.

The altar was finished, but its completion was more a beginning than an end. I had a place of my own—the private retreat I'd wanted for the twenty-five years since first reading of Jung's tower—where I could better commune with the Divine, invite the transcendent into my home, and make my inner life tangible and visible. My altar welcomed me to explore *its* uses which were really *my* own. It offered freedom and limitless possibilities of expression.

I dedicated the finished altar by arranging on it a wedding anniversary tableau: photographs of my wife and me through twentysome years of marriage; a vase of daisies, signature flowers of our relationship; two candles in antique holders; and a bottle of champagne and two glasses. The red cedar backdrop reflected candle glow in its dark varnished depths. The glazed yellow tile shone cheerfully. The altar stood gracefully tall.

Experiments and Expressions

My passion for building quickly transformed into enthusiasm for finding different ways to put it to use. I designed the unfolding triptych lid to display small pictures and prints. Wanting a semipermanent tableau, I commissioned my eighty-year-old dad to paint on four small panels: a tree in each of the four seasons. I cherish those panels. Whenever I look at those trees hanging in series on my altar, they invoke feelings and memories of nature, love, family, and the passage and cycles of time that choke me with good emotion. The paintings are a legacy—panels as sacred as those I had once contemplated in the sanctuary at Chimayo, New Mexico.

Through the winter months after I built my altar, I had an ongoing arrangement: ten daffodil bulbs that came as a Christmas gift from a faraway friend. I put the bulbs in a shallow yellow pot, forcing their blooms. I placed two tapers in holders on either side of the pot. Whenever I felt gloomy or tired of winter, I lit the candles and enjoyed the sight of the growing and eventually blooming daffodils. The ritual lifted my spirits and buoyed my hope. The flowers also reminded me of the giver, a friend who lived half a continent away.

I experimented with other arrangements in observance of holidays and seasonal occasions. I set my altar with a vase of red and white carnations, candles in silver holders given as wedding gifts years ago, and a card to mark Valentine's Day. On the vernal equinox, the beginning of spring, I lit a cheerful vase of forsythia buds with a half dozen sparkling votives. The forsythia stayed on my altar until the last bloom fell. When the lilacs bloomed later that spring, I placed a fragrant bouquet of them on my altar and read Walt Whitman's haunting elegy to Lincoln. It begins with lines that pierce my heart: "When lilacs last in the dooryard bloom'd. . . ."

As spring passed I gathered branches and flowers to place in vases on my altar. I gave these bouquets no more intention than bringing nature's beauty indoors. I received an unexpected bonus when I realized they heightened my awareness of the passing seasons. I felt more intimately connected with nature's rhythms. My altar opened my eyes and sharpened my sensitivities to much in nature I'd simply ignored.

I fashioned altar arrangements to express private spiritual aspirations or concerns. At a Sunday service I read from a contemporary book that used the metaphor of a Buddhist monk's begging bowl. In response I received marvelous gifts from two artisans in my congregation: a hand-pressed pottery bowl and a small woven basket. Each was perfectly suited for my altar. They symbolized a spiritual attitude toward which I aspire—openness and receptivity to life's gifts. On many mornings, before going off to work, I would place the empty basket on my altar to inspire this spiritual attitude. I eventually wrote a prose meditation to express this spiritual attitude. This was the first of what I came to call *devotions*: readings to correspond to my altar arrangements.

Feeling generally grumpy and disconnected in late spring, tired at the end of the church year, I gathered mementos and photographs of many friends and put them on my altar. As object after object evoked a relationship, I remembered a favorite poem, "A Garden of Friends," by a colleague, Max Coots. I reread that poem as I looked on this special altar and began to recover my equilibrium and sense of connectedness.

My altar encouraged me to change. The effort and focus of arranging an altar was a special sort of commitment to my inner self as well as the Divine. I left an arrangement as long as necessary to remind me to keep a particular spiritual attitude.

Within the first six months of exploring the place of my own that was my altar, I found that it had become indispensable to my spiritual life. It was a refuge and a place of comfort. It provided an incredible freedom of expression. Its daily presence confronted me: "How will you use me? I'm ready and able to meet whatever it is you need!" Even when I let it rest, I did so because rest was what *I* needed. It stimulated creativity. It connected me with the flow of time and the succession of nature. Its beauty related to a greater beauty, which I experienced as the living relationship with the transcendent I craved. In form and function it helped to fulfill what William Channing Gannett in "House Beautiful" had called "domestication of the infinite." Because of my altar, my home was more home-like—filled with the best of my being and aspiring to the Divine through beautiful things, virtuous activity, transcendent truths.

My altar was a *home altar*, not only in location but also in its effect on my domestic life. I was gratified that my wife occasionally used it to celebrate our relationship by setting up an arrangement, as a gift to me.

Living by the Meaning of Things

I had quickly realized that my altar would never be entirely my own creation, though it would always be a place of my own. When I began to describe and show it to friends, many of those friends gave me thoughtful gifts with my altar in mind. My altar seemed to have a life of its own, at least a life beyond what I brought to it. My altar had gotten into the souls of others, and they wanted to get their souls onto my altar—not selfishly, but through their relationship with me. I realized how this enriched the already complex meaning of my altar through the language of objects. And I remembered what Antoine de St. Exupery once wrote: "We live, not by things, but by the meaning of things."

Friends gave me a stone from a Florida beach that looked like a mother curled around a child, an oval, hand-turned walnut vase, shells gathered along the Texas Gulf coast, a stained-glass sculpture of a winter tree, a handblown glass bud vase, a cardinal's bright red feather, a ginkgo leaf preserved in a frame, and, of course, a variety of stones. The gift givers each inevitably said, "When I saw this I thought of you and your altar." Placed on my altar, these objects inevitably reminded me of each of the givers.

Occasionally I would find an object in a shop perfectly suited for my sacred space. I bought a turned aspen base to support a three-inch-wide column candle, six frosted-glass votive holders, two freestanding photo frames, and a small silver bowl to use exclusively on my new home altar. I also gathered things from what we already owned: candlesticks, vases, and bowls. In a matter of months I acquired a cache of special altar objects that had acquired ritual significance. I handled these things more lovingly than before, which I took as a subtle lesson in awareness.

Devotions

In the same way that I gathered the altar objects, I collected written materials, which turned into a book of devotions. Whenever I looked upon an altar arrangement I'd created, a favorite quotation or poetic meditation popped into mind—often one I'd written for an occasion during the twenty years of my ministry. Over the years I'd also acquired a wealth of resources from colleagues I admired and by a whole range of other writers.

Sometimes an altar arrangement would remind me of a personal experience, and I would write a special piece in tribute. As the words flowed, I found that my interest in finding a language beyond words, through my altar, was really an attempt to set free the words and the ideas they conveyed. I loved words, their music as well as their relationship to imagination. I found words so much the better for their association with the objects arranged on my altar. It wasn't that words explained the objects. It was more that the objects and their arrangements gave more meaning to the words.

I began to pair altar arrangements and devotional writings.

I didn't always need devotional words; the careful placement of things was often enough. However, words often seemed to focus my intentions in creating a particular altar; and the words, of course, had their own associations. Words connected me to my younger self, to other persons and places, further enriching the altar experience. The words were also portable. I could take them with me into the day, while my home altar remained at my house.

My collection of devotions naturally took the shape of a yearly cycle, because many had seasonal and holiday themes. I could return to a devotion season after season and feel a familiar comfort, a synchronicity with nature's larger rhythms. Maintaining a spirit of freedom and creativity, I didn't, however, feel obligated to follow a strict seasonal cycle. I always kept in mind that my altar should be an outer expression of my inner spirituality first and foremost. This approach increased my own self-awareness, and I was better able to monitor and adjust my spiritual good health.

A home altar had given me the place of my own I had long wanted—the place where I continue to realize an ever-richer spiritual life. It's a sacred place of creativity, connection, communication, and commitment.

You, too, can have a place of your own to enrich your spirituality. The beginnings are probably already in front of you.

Your Home Altar

L ook around your home and find the places—a windowsill, a corner of a desk, a bureau or dresser top—you've claimed spontaneously as your own with arrangements of meaningful objects. Why are these things important to you? Answering that question can be the beginning of a spiritual journey.

Through photographs we remember and honor special people in our lives—family, friends, and heroes. Souvenirs and mementos connect you to other places and days. Natural objects—a feather, tumbled beach stones, seashells, dried flowers—have beauty that intimates the order and beauty of Creation. A cherished book or a poem written in calligraphy may inspire you. A small sculpture, a postcard of a favorite painting, a figurine suggest the beauty of life around you. A cross or crucifix, a statue of a saint, a small Buddha, or Taoism's yin and yang within a circle signify your religious traditions or inclinations. Candlelight adds a warm glow, a little romance, and a tacit invocation or blessing.

All of these tangible things carry intangible

meanings. They remind, signify, and symbolize. They are more than personal. They uplift and bless your relationships with yourself, others, aspects of nature, Creation, and God. Their beauty comes from a greater beauty. The choices you make and how you choose to arrange these objects are creative acts that flow from an irresistible urge. Creating these places of your own is a spiritual activity, because they reflect a greater design.

The places you claim in your home with arrangements of special objects are sacred spaces. They bless your whole home. They wait, patient and always ready, to fulfill your spiritual needs. They are the personal altars you've already created.

Domesticating the Infinite

Now that I have recognized and created an altar of my own, I recognize sacred spaces everywhere I go. It is the rare home in which I have not seen a personal altar, though those who make them probably wouldn't call them altars. They take many forms and are found in a variety of places.

A midlife woman I know who maintains an elegant suburban home uses a waist-high Chinese console, its top curved gracefully at the sides to display framed black and white childhood photographs of grandparents, parents, and herself. This altar, dedicated to her ancestry and early years, commands a prominent wall in the living room.

A man's home office, an extra bedroom, has two large desks. One desk overflows with mementos he keeps at arm's reach, so his glance may fall over the display as he works. Occasionally one of the objects twinkles at him like a star in heaven's panoply. The objects include stones, candles, a medal from his first vocal competitions, feathers, two little boxes, one filled with shells and the other with foreign coins, small carvings of birds, a ceramic bowl formed by a child's hand, and an egg he hollowed out, carefully cracked, resealed with a coded message inside. In college he had shared a house with seven other men; they called such displays their "areas." But he'd been answering his "nesting instinct" since boyhood.

A friend deeply involved in Native American spirituality has converted an empty-nest bedroom of her Victorian house into a room of her own. The whole room is sacred space. It contains several ceremonial drums, a meditation fountain, framed pictures and sayings. There are several specific altars. A curio cabinet is divided into small niches filled with small carved stone fetishes—totem animals that each have deep significance for her.

A single woman living in a modern townhouse devotes a long mantel in her dining room to vintage portraits of ancestors and her immediate family, as well as snapshots of her with friends. Among the photographs she manages to find space for significant little things: dried flowers, postcards, stones, champagne corks, and a variety of other mementos, plus several candles. This jumbled whole contrasts sharply with the spare, modern lines of her furniture.

Parents who have children often select a place in their bedroom as a private, sacred space and arrange objects on a dresser or windowsill. A woman I know keeps her treasures safe from her young children's curious hands. She reserves the top shelf of a bedroom bookcase for her treasures, including the most sacred object in her life: a cedar flute made by an aged grandfather she met late in his life. He told her that, though he had once thought he "made it for no reason," he was sure now that the Creator had directed him to make the flute for the granddaughter he'd never known but would soon meet.

A working mother with two young children reserves a bedside table as her altar. Her small house overflows with toys, books, and clothes—all the stuff of contemporary domestic life. Though her bedside altar is still functional—for instance, it has a reading lamp with a stained-glass shade given as a wedding present—she arranges on it a small box containing cards with one word meditations, ordinary gifts her children are always giving her, one or two recent greeting cards, and a natural wood frame in which she places a current photograph of a particular family member she wants to honor. The shelf underneath holds meditation books. Her small altar is the one space she can claim as her own—a tranquil space in the midst of often chaotic family life. It's also a barometer for her state of mind. When it becomes cluttered with discarded tissues and other domestic detritus, she knows it's time to be more attentive to her own needs.

A retired friend with a city apartment, who has scaled back the things he owns, positions the desk where he writes poetry in front of a window that looks toward Lake Michigan. On the windowsill he places objects of poetic inspiration: a bonsai tree he is training and a row of books by his favorite poets, including Basho, the Japanese haiku master.

Next to her low dresser, my wife, Ellie, has attached a small shelf adorned with autumn leaves. On the shelf is a photograph of our now grown daughter walking at eleven months and a glazed pot with a lid dating from Katy's junior high years.

A homemaker, who complains with good humor that she spends too much time at the kitchen sink, has turned a nearby wall into a vertical altar. On it she groups feathers, a sunset photograph taken by a special friend, a gift hat, a group snapshot of her woman's group, poems, words to music, the Prayer of Saint Francis, and a favorite picture of her daughter.

Your Home Altar

There's no right way or place for setting up a home altar. What's right depends on your circumstances, sensibilities, and intentions.

You might begin to explore the possibilities of a home altar by identifying an altar you've created naturally and then begin to use it intentionally. However, I believe there's much to be gained by dedicating a special piece of furniture as a place of your own. Perhaps you'll graduate to an altar you create from scratch. Designing and building one as I did can be time-consuming and simply isn't possible for everyone. But you can utilize a piece of furniture you already own as your home altar, using it as is or modifying it, by refinishing it or painting it imaginatively. Such attention imbues the altar with your spirit.

You may find the idea of a home altar to be such an exciting addition to your personal spiritual life that you want a very special piece of furniture, perhaps one seasoned by age and use. Searching for that special piece can mark the beginning of a fulfilling spiritual quest. Visualize your ideal home altar and visit antique and secondhand stores in search of its realization. Or go with no image in mind, trusting that you will know when you've found your altar. An old occasional table, bookshelf, small cabinet, or desk will speak to your spiritual imagination. The patina of age, dents and nicks, the understanding that many hands have touched it give an old piece character you can't resist. You've found your personal altar! Be free to decorate it to make it more your own.

Exercise your decorative skills, with a piece of unfinished furniture such as cabinets, desks, tables, shelves. Most stores that sell ready-to-finish pieces have a selection of suitable and inexpensive possibilities. Give your imagination free reign in painting and decorating such a piece. One of my favorite small altars is a small pine shelf that friend and artist, Marya Veeck, painted with dark colors and autumn leaves, which my wife placed in an alcove above her low dresser. Even if your home is crowded with belongings, there is almost always room for a shelf. Why not paint and decorate it yourself?

A Sacred Space

Your choice of an altar will depend in part on where in your home you plan to put it, as well as the sort of objects you'd like to arrange on it. If privacy from a busy household is an issue, try the bedroom, study, or home office. If your home altar customarily has a lot of things on it, it might make sense to locate it in a less public part of the house. You might want your altar to be near you as you sleep, by your side as you work, in your kitchen where you eat most of your meals.

I prefer my altar to be an integral piece of furniture in the center of my living space—a harmonious element in the harmonious whole of my home—on which simple seasonal and occasional objects are arranged, most often flowers and candles. My altar is in my living room to one side of my fireplace. Such an altar in a common area of the house—living room, dining room, family room, kitchen, or den—beautifies as it provides a familiar spiritual focus for you and your family. Even when I haven't set it with special objects, when the lid is down, my altar still has a spiritual presence for me. It's *my* altar and it awaits my use.

Keep in mind, you can have more than one altar—a very personal one and then one that your family and guests can enjoy; or one you set with a somewhat permanent display and then one you change regularly in rhythm with the occasions of your life.

The Language of Objects

I've collected beautiful and useful things for the arrangements I've fashioned to celebrate and observe a yearly cycle, in conjunction with the weekly devotions I've created. I prefer simple arrangements to better focus my intentions. Occasionally I find something so perfect it was clearly made for my altar. My intentions for these things and their purpose on my altar have imbued these carefully chosen objects with meaning. I've found that choosing, gathering, and keeping items for my altar is in itself a satisfying ritual.

I've gathered a number of vases, each of the right proportions for my altar, including bud vases that are designed to hold a single flower. I've given special attention to candleholders: a turned aspen base for a three-inch column candle; sets of candleholders—wood, ceramic, and silver; clear and colored glass votive candleholders. Friends have given small pottery bowls they've turned. And I cherish a small basket in a Native American design, which another friend made for me. You can interchange a variety of vases, candles and candleholders, and small bowls and baskets so your altar arrangements are always new but continue to have a comforting familiarity. Small cabinets or chests make excellent home altars, because they also provide storage space for items you will use with your altar's changing arrangements.

You will surely have your own special objects such as the objects you've gathered for your natural altars. As your altar takes you through the seasons and occasions you will accumulate, as I've accumulated, new altar objects.

Recently I've added aroma to my altar devotions. Scented candles are handy and you can match the scent to the occasion. I'm fond of a clever scent machine that was a gift for my altar: It's a small geode cut in half to form a bowl in which aromatic oils are poured; a tripod-like metal base suspends the geode over a tea lite; the flame of the tea lite heats the oil to release the oil's aroma.

To frame your altar, you might want to consider a background similar to the lid of my altar, which unfolds into a triptych. For example, a simple folding screen can be easily crafted from sections of foam board joined with tape and then covered with fabric, drawn upon, or decorated with a collage of pictures or photographs.

When completed, your altar will feel right, because it's your creation. Don't be surprised if you continually adapt and refine your design. As you adapt it, you'll begin to know how important your home altar is in your spiritual life. It is a center to which you can always return and restore your soul, while experiencing a wonderful freedom and creativity to follow the beckonings of your spirit.

Using Your Altar

How you choose to use your altar can follow several paths. Begin by exploring arrangements that focus your intentions and inspire you—the simpler the better, at first. You might meditate on those arrangements in a mindful way for five or ten minutes, perhaps beginning by lighting a candle and closing by extinguishing the candle. In addition, you might recite a special meditation or prayer—the Lord's Prayer, St. Francis's Prayer, Reinhold Neibhur's "Serenity Prayer," or Max Ehrmann's "Desiderata"—read a selection from scripture or a prayer book.

In time, you might begin to create your own personal devotions. Gather favorite writings for particular occasions and observances, integrating the words with your altar arrangements. My altar took me on this path, and I developed a yearlong cycle of devotions. These devotions, included in this book, illustrate some of the many possibilities for fashioning a rich devotional life.

There are days when I don't want words, and on those days I arrange my altar and revel in the silence. There are days when I must have words to enrich the meanings of the objects I have arranged, and I use devotions. There are days when a poem, reading, and even a musical selection inspires me, and I create an altar to portray a meaning. There are days when I just want a nondemanding beauty, and I enjoy a bouquet of flowers or flickering candlelight on my altar. There are even days when I don't want anything at all on my altar, and I leave it empty.

Just as there is no right way or place for setting up a home altar, neither is there a right way to use it. You decide what's right for you. What that is will probably evolve and progress with experience.

I always strive to be genuine and spontaneous—true to my immediate urges and needs. Nevertheless, I'm glad I've created a cycle of devotions to keep me in tune with the seasons and unfolding year—to buoy me when I'm weary and occasionally prod me out of complacency.

Devotions to Use and Adapt

I offer you the fifty-two devotions I've created. You can use or edit them to suit your own sensibilities. They will help you see the possibilities and, I hope, inspire you to create your own.

The devotions progress week by week through the seasons. The themes vary: seasonal observances, holidays, celebrations, spiritual disciplines, reflections or meditations, attitude adjustments, and self-development. Generally they affirm and are thankful, evoking moods of the season and day, and lead toward connection and communion.

I believe the ordinary and everyday is holy. If only we could recognize it and try to make it more so. My devotions are grounded in a belief in this natural holiness—this imminence of miracle that you can bring into your home and into your life, and from this center take its spirit out into the world.

Each devotion includes a suggested arrangement of objects to place on your own altar. I prefer devotions that have an esthetic simplicity, because I appreciate simplicity in my private devotions. One or a few objects on your altar will help you keep a sharp focus, and your mind will be less prone to wander.

Remember that in using your altar you seek personal authenticity, intimacy, and integrity. In this regard don't be bound by my suggestions. Be creative in adapting. Set free your active imagination. The possibilities are a kind of spiritual play that includes the pleasure of art.

Sacred Time for Sacred Space

Whenever you use your home altar, a little ritual to open and close the devotion helps to separate this contemplative time from the rest of the day. I generally light and extinguish a candle. A bell or chimes serve the same purpose.

Consider, too, the time of day best suited to use your altar. I like my altar and devotions to enthuse and guide me as I begin a new day, so I am generally drawn to mornings. But on certain days, when I feel expansive and enraptured by life, afternoon has its appeal. And when I'm frazzled at the end of a busy day, my home altar soothes me in the evening. I can change my altar throughout the day, too—a cheerful and fresh bouquet of flowers in the morning to welcome the day and to last until night when I replace them with a single candle burning in a darkened room to beckon sleep.

This book, *A Place of Your Own*, encourages you, through the beauty and intention of a home altar and the practice of weekly devotions, to discover the possibilities of *spiritual at-homeness*. In this process your home is both a cause and an effect. It is here, as William Channing Gannett wrote, that you "domesticate the infinite," infusing your life with value and meaning. What you create in your home goes with you as you step out into the world and meet the day.

A Year of Devotions

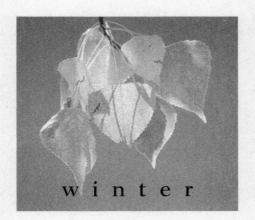

winter

Place a photograph or print of a winter landscape, candles, and perhaps a whimsical glass snow globe scene on your altar. Arrange evergreen or holly branches around them. I burn scented candles or a stick of balsam incense.

Winter needs all the help it can get: That is my first thought when the days grow short and the cold weather has settled in for a long stay. As I grow older I find winter increasingly difficult to enjoy.

When I think about it, I realize winter doesn't need help. Actually, I need all the help I can get in order to deal creatively with winter. In the scheme of the seasons, winter is part of the natural order, possessing, therefore, inherent goodness. It is my attitude that needs adjustment. Greta W. Crosby's counsel about the "pregnant negativities" of the season helps me enter and endure winter with a more positive outlook.

Let us not wish away the winter. It is a season to itself, not simply the way to spring.

*When trees rest, growing no leaves, gathering
no light, they lie in sky and trace themselves del-
icately against dawns and sunsets.*

*The clarity and brilliance of the winter sky
delight. The loom of fog softens edges, lulls the eyes
and ears of the quiet, awakens by risk the unquiet. A low dark
sky can snow, emblem of individuality, liberality, and aggre-
gate power. Snow invites to contemplation and to sport.*

Winter is a table set with ice and starlight.

*Winter dark tends to warm light: fire and candle; winter
cold to hugs and huddles; winter want to gifts and sharing;
winter danger to visions, plans, and common endeavoring—
and the zest of narrow escapes; winter tedium to merry-
making.*

*Let us therefore praise winter, rich in beauty, challenge,
and pregnant negativities.*

I need to draw on my own experiences, too, to remind myself of the beauty in winter I've seen. Yes, I've encountered
much beauty in winter. In earlier years, when a long, cold and
snowy Northern winter was a novelty, even the most common
images elated me. I praised those images in a meditation.

WINTER IMAGES

*A graceful evergreen dusted with fresh snow.
The long smooth taper of an icicle—
a crystal drop suspended from its tip.*

A scarlet cardinal flashing through a gray thicket.
A billow of steam rising from a tall factory smokestack.
A pale evening sky washed with yellows and reds.
A solitary tree poised on the horizon.
The rapid exhalation of warm breath in frigid air.
Cheeks flushed, ruddy from cold.
Thin sunlight spilling over a rough tree trunk.
Delicate ice-crystal etchings on window glass.
Vivid flames dancing on burning logs:

These images—
and so many more—
I love in winter.

Not to appreciate winter's possibilities means the loss of a significant portion of your life. Winter offers unique gifts. And winter also challenges you to find *your* meaning—the defining attributes of a human being.

WINTER'S BLESSINGS

In this winter I wish for you
Happy Holidays: busy but not too hectic; rich with friends and family; and at least one occasion to think, reflect, and discover your own sense of Peace on Earth.
The promise of a New Year and all the good intentions you can muster; plus the personal grace not to feel guilty when practice falls short of resolve.

Edward Searl

Good books and long nights.

Aromas to quicken the memory: moth balls and wet wool; wood smoke in the night; balsam pine; baking bread.

Visions to penetrate the soul: a staunch, solitary tree— branches splayed against a gray sky; colored lights on an evergreen in an inky night; heavily padded children with flushed cheeks and red, drippy noses; the compelling sight of your own breath on the coldest day of the year.

A blizzard that cancels your plans, reminding you that some things are beyond your control and there are powers to which you must yield.

Sounds to stir your emotions: frigid gales howling in the night, making you glad for your bed; wind moaning in the pines, filling you with deep satisfaction for companionship; the reassuring roar and scrape of a snowplow clearing the road; the first trickle of melting snow, sharpening your senses.

Endurance and creativity and hope: the will to shovel snow; the delight of catching a single snowflake on the tip of your tongue; and the sure knowledge that spring will come— no matter how long winter lingers.

Yes, winter blessing for you,
From November's tentative flakes of snow
Through the vernal return of the buzzards to Hinckley, Ohio.

A Meditation in Eleven Candles

Match eleven candles by color to the eleven candles in this devotion. Arrange those candles in an assortment of holders. I use wooden, silver, pottery, and glass holders and the candles vary in height. Consider sprinkling Christmas potpourri around the candles. A festive perfume carried by the convection of burning candles will fill the room.

December contains the holiest nights of the year—the Winter Solstice, Christmas, Hanukkah, and for twenty-six years, Kwanza. This devotion works especially well at night, perhaps before dinner. Similar to the Hanukkah or Kwanza candle-lighting rituals, you might begin by lighting one candle a night starting on December twenty-first, Solstice Eve, and ending with the lighting of the eleventh candle on New Year's Eve.

Eleven Candles to Celebrate
the Holidays

We light the first candle for the Sun, to remind us that we are enchanted stardust—of Nature and never removed from it.

We affirm that the seasons turn. We are assured that our fragile, miracle life endures through the seasons and the generations.

This candle signifies the many festivals of the Winter Solstice. We imagine roaring bonfires that burned long ago on hilltops to coax the retreating Sun to return. We recall that this is the birthday of Natalis Invicti, the unconquered God, Mithra to the ancient Persians, the Sun personified at the Winter Solstice.

In this flame is the unspoken meaning of Cosmic Creation: vast distances, subatomic and cosmic reactions and attractions, and evolution arching toward life, consciousness, and self-consciousness.

We light a second candle to acknowledge Hanukkah and a Jewish heritage that is a wellspring of Western Civilization. The Hanukkah flame is not the Sun symbolized, a reenactment of ancient Solstice rites. This is a flame of human faith and of unswerving conviction. It recalls an ageless struggle against all forces that oppress the human soul. It is a yearning for justice. It is the freedom that stirs in every human heart— especially the freedom to worship as each of us wishes.

It signifies a faith that we are sustained—miraculously—if we live reverently and courageously, devoted to that which is beautiful, good, and true. With such a mind nothing can dissuade us from our faith. Its heat anneals us to tradition and principle.

We light a third candle to honor the Earth, our home. The greenery of the season—garlands and ropes of cedar, wreaths of balsam, fir trees—have long served as symbols of the tenacity of Nature.

Greens graced the Roman holiday of Saturnalia. They provided refuge for the little people believed in by ancient Brits—sprites, elves, and brownies—who took refuge among the boughs brought indoors when the outdoors turned to icy stone.

Always the message of the greens is unmistakable: Life endures the harshest seasons, because the fir tree stays ever green, bows to the wind, and bends under the snow, but never succumbs to Winter.

We light a fourth candle in memory of all the Ancient and Modern Festivals of Midwinter that compel us to joy, so rich and wide that not even the fabled twelve days of Christmas can contain them: Babylonian Zagmuk, Roman Saturnalia, North Europe's Yule, the Angli's Mother Night, Medieval Noel, Victorian Christmas, the Christmases of our childhood.

Through this flame, let us see that it is good to be generous, to seek the company and bonhomie of family and friends, to feast, generally be merry, to suspend reality, be childlike, and loving—above all loving.

We light a fifth candle for the Nativity Story: of the love of a mother as she carried her child in her body, bearing a mother's knowledge that this child was conceived by a love so immense that this child will be the promised child. Of a tiring journey met with such indifference that a woman about to give birth and her worried husband had to take shelter in a manger. Of the humble birth of a child whose compassion, wisdom, and sense of justice changed the course of civilization. Of humble shepherds and great seers, alike sharing the knowledge that eluded a King. This is a story of Incarnation—the Divine, the Spirit within Creation seeking human form—taking place in the birth of every child. Always we wonder, will this child be the child to save our troubled world?

We light a sixth candle not to forget the Meek, whom a wise man enigmatically declared "will inherit the earth." While the exalted Magi sought the child by following a star, the revelation was first given to humble shepherds, who, we imagine, were most receptive and, curiously, most deserving. It was to humble parents that the Christ child was born.

So Christmas reminds us of the humble, the innocent, and the young. It points to the oppressed. In this season we are pierced by the plights of the homeless, the hungry, the impoverished, the abused, the oppressed, the ill as we are at no other season. We respond with acts of compassion, charity, and justice.

We light a seventh candle for Gifts. It is like a dance, this giving and receiving at the Holidays. It is an allegory of what we human beings do for one another throughout the year. We represent the gift-giver as a Wise Elder—Befana and Saint Nicholas, because gift-giving is human wisdom. Gift-giving unites us, often across miles during the Holidays. Be-

cause the gifts we give are carefully chosen and eagerly anticipated, they take on special, ritual significance.

Really the greatest gifts of Christmas are the simplest, humblest gifts, the sort that can't be wrapped, ribboned, and bowed. These are the gifts of song, of grace, of beauty, of joy, and, of course, of love.

We light an eighth candle in love of Children. They are our generational solstice—our hope and confidence that not just our being, the personal life we love, but all that we declare to be precious in our world, will renew, survive, and even grow greater in our children that it has lived in us.

Humankind is born anew with every child. A child's eyes see for the first time. All is fresh, innocent, and wondering; so all appears to children as it really is—a miracle!

Children respond to the Holidays spontaneously, that is, naturally. Adults need only remember to recapture the childlike within them to receive the blessings of the season.

We praise childlikeness, proclaiming this is the spirit in which to experience the season—accepting, expecting, wondering, marveling.

We light a ninth candle in hope of Peace on Earth, the mythic Angel Song. We wish peace of self, that each of us, if only for the season, will be free of self-doubt and inner torment. We wish peace between one another, feeling, if only for the season, the friendliness, the kinship, and fellow-feeling that makes us glad and sustains our spirits. We wish peace among people everywhere—among nations, cultures, ethnic groups, races, classes, and families.

Fears, resentments, angers, hurts, envies, jealousies, all petty annoyances have no place among us in this season. Remember that peace on earth is conditioned by goodwill. Peace begins with you and me.

We light a tenth candle for Family. There are many different kinds of families—all bound by love, need, and nurture.

There are the families we choose, including our beloved friends. And there is our Great Family—all of humanity— where all races, all nations, all creeds, all superficial differences dissolve into One Heart, One Mind, One Soul, One Humanity.

Every family is the Holy Family.

And we light an eleventh candle to keep and build Memories: For memories of Christmases past, with all their ambivalences, but mostly in the subdued light that time casts, weaving days gone by in soft golden threads. We remember old friends and family members now departed.

And for the Christmas now and memories we are making, not just for ourself alone, but for those whose lives touch our lives, we light this final candle. May the magic of the season transform our lives through the Love that was always, is now, and will never end.

Look at the burning candles. They symbolize all that comes together in this Season: ancient festivals, Hanukkah, Christmas, but more, something in the timeless human heart that needs and finds—a coming home to a truer self and a reality that in its dream likeness is a vision that guides us through the year until the holidays come again.

Place two candleholders on your altar. In one place a nub of a candle with only an inch or two of wax. In the second holder place an unburnt taper. Light the shorter candle. At the conclusion of the devotion light the new candle from the burning nub. Extinguish the nub.

Time is a great mystery. We speak of a space-time continuum and of time as the fourth dimension. The theory of relativity tells us time slows down as we (if we could) approach the speed of light. Now, thanks to computer-generated virtual realities, we speak of "real" and "virtual" time.

Earth time has always been marked by recurring cycles. "The wind goeth toward the south, and turneth about unto the north; it whirleth about continually, and the wind returneth again according to his circuits. . . . The thing that hath been, it is that which shall be; and that which is done is that which shall be done: and there is no new thing under the sun." (KJV, Eccles. 1:6 & 9) Ecclesiastes declares. The ancient Celts divided the year in half according to agricultural cycles. The ancient Hebrews calculated time by the cycles of the moon. The Jewish New Year, Rosh Hashanah, usually falls in the month of September. Easter, a Christian Passover, is determined by the moon's phases, so it changes from year to year as we reckon time by a solar calendar. January 1, though near the winter solstice, is still an arbitrary beginning of a new year. Still, New Year's Day marks a beginning—one necessarily prefaced by a sentimental song to "days gone by."

CONTROLLING TIME

When I was young there was a neighbor who, at the stroke of midnight every January 1, lifted a shotgun to the sky and fired a blazing blast of buckshot into the infinite darkness. I couldn't figure out whether he was trying to kill the old year or whether he was welcoming the New Year.

Most of us make noise at the stroke of midnight every January 1. I'm still undecided whether the noise we make on New Year's Eve is to drive away the old or to herald in the new.

We both banish and welcome time at this annual witching hour. We desire a fresh start, a clean slate for our lives. We lay aside our unhappiness, disappointments, and failures. They belong to the past—the past we drive away with a raucous cacophony of noise. We welcome the hope and promise of a new year, showing our joy in the prospect by making the loudest reveling noises possible.

So we fool ourselves into believing that we can control

time, that we can draw one chapter to an end and make another begin. The funny thing is, it seems to work.

May the anticipation and hope and promise that the New Year brings be always before us.

The old year is forever dying; the New Year is forever being born.

Such an auspicious and monumental beginning as New Year's calls for a prayer.

NEW YEAR PRAYER

May you find
the New Year—
with its full cycle of seasons—
Time enough for you:

Time enough
to laugh when you are happy,
to cry when you are sad;
Time enough
to strive and succeed,
to rest and be renewed;
Time enough
to discover deeply,
to give freely;
Time enough
to love selflessly,

to be loved satisfyingly;
Time enough
for you to be
your essential self
And to enter eternity
by living fully
in the moment—
One with self,
One with others,
One with Life itself.

A Hymn to Sleep

Set your altar with a single candle. After you light it, turn the lights in the room down low or off.

Though grouped with winter devotions, this devotion can be used throughout the year. It is an affirmation, as well as a declaration of trust and faith. Begin by lighting a candle on your altar. For a few minutes stare at the burning flame, relax your body, and your mind.

A HYMN TO SLEEP

1
Darkness has descended.
And the Night beckons,
Whispering from the darkness,
Whispering from the deep:

Don't worry. Don't fear.
Don't resist.
Be at rest.
I bring you peace.

2

Be calmed.
Be soothed.
Be healed.
Let sleep come
in long, slow waves,
Long slow waves,
Lifted by the darkness,
Rolling from the Sea of Self.

3

The Night is a grace.
The darkness is a comforting presence.

4

Like the arms of a Mother,
Like the arms of a Father,
Gathering an only child,
I'm gathered
by the arms of Night.
I give myself to the darkness
And to the keeping of Creation.

5

The long rolling waves
that are in me
Rise and swell

A Place of Your Own

To wash away
all anxieties,
all vexations,
all distresses,
all hurt and pain.
all insecurities,
all worries about tomorrow,
Soothing,
Comforting,
Healing
My body and my mind.

6
My soul is at rest.

7
I let go—gently. I yield to the sleep
rising from the Sea of Self.
I let go—fearlessly.
I'm gathered into loving arms.

8
And now,
Giving myself to sleep,
the sweet elixir of Night,
I whisper this prayer into the darkness:

Edward Searl

Be with me and
Sustain me, Life.
Bring me Peace.
And let me wake again.

Extinguish the candle.

The Treasures of the Snow

There are few sights more pristine and bright, as well as strangely peaceful, as a morning snowscape following a storm. Select a photograph or print of such a snowscape. Place votives in glass containers around it.

Each of us creates our own happiness; we nourish the meaning in our individual lives. Personality matters: whether we're an optimist or a pessimist. And our spiritual liveliness comes to play, too. I think that whether we see the proverbial glass as half empty or half full insinuates our spiritual health. In this regard, how we "see" snow indicates whether or not we have "spiritual eyes."

WHAT DO YOU SEE?

The same winter's day
With the same winter scenes
After a snowfall—
What do you see?

Is there beauty
in the clear, thin light;
in the precise gray shadows
splayed on the clean snow;
in the graceful powder
icing the trees;
in the bare asymmetry
of tangled branches?

Or do you find only that which is
cold and austere;
drab and dull;
stark and uninviting?

Can you wonder
at the miraculous infinitude
of six-faceted crystals?
Or must you curse snow inconveniences:
slippery streets and sodden socks?

Do you hear peace in the muffled quiet?
Or is there a frigid lifelessness
echoing for you?

The same winter's day
With the same winter's scenes—
For some there is beauty and grace,
For others there is emptiness and despair.

What is there for you
In this winter's day?

The Book of Job from the Old Testament asked a similar question.

Hast thou entered into the treasures of the snow? or hast thou
seen the treasures of the hail, [KJV, Job 38:22]

Henry David Thoreau saw divinity in snow. And he made a logical connection that divinity was in human nature.

The thin snow now driving from the north and lodging on
my coat consists of those beautiful star crystals. . . . Nature is
full of genius, full of the divinity; so that not a snowflake
escapes its fashioning hand.
    The same law that shapes the earth-star shapes the snow-
star. As surely as the petals of a flower are fixed, each of these
countless snow-stars comes whirling to earth, pronouncing
thus, with emphasis, the number six. Order, cosmos!
    What a world we live in, where myriads of these little
disks, so beautiful of the most prying eye, are whirled down
on every traveler's coat, the observant and unobservant, and
on the restless squirrels' fur, and on the far-stretching fields
and forests, the wooded dells, and the mountaintops. Far, far
away from the haunts of man, they roll down some little slope,
fall over and come to their bearings, and melt or lose their
beauty in the mass, ready anon to swell some little rill with

their contribution, and so, at last the universal ocean from which they came. There they lie, like the wreck of chariot wheels after a battle in the skies. Meanwhile the meadow mouse shoves them aside in his gallery, the schoolboy casts them in his snowball, or the woodman's sled slides smoothly over them, these glorious spangles, the sweepings of heaven's floor.

And they all sing, melting as they sing of the mysteries of the number six—six, six, six. He takes up the waters of the sea in his hand leaving the salt; He disperses it in mist through the skies; He recollects and sprinkles it like grain in six-rayed snowy stars over the earth, there to lie till He dissolves its bonds again.

Thanks to Thoreau, whenever I marvel at the infinitude and beauty of snowflakes, my mind leaps in elation at the uniqueness and beauty of humankind.

CRYSTALLINE BEAUTY

Who I am,
Who you are
Is something precious.

We, who can marvel,
at the crystalline beauty
of snowflakes,

A Place of Your Own

> Can't we marvel at the infinite beauty
> of one another?
>
> Each person is unique—
> as perfect in being
> as a six-sided snow crystal
> is perfect.
>
> Yet person is like person,
> As crystal is like crystal.
> In our humanness
> Our uniqueness is transformed
> but never lost—
> As the uniqueness of a snow crystal
> is never lost in a bank of snow.
>
> May each come to know
> the beauty and perfection of self.
> And may we know the possibility
> of our common humanity,
> As we grow—alone and together—
> into our humanness and our humanity.

For me the cardinal, not the robin, is the genuine harbinger of spring. One day in late January or early February I hear the male cardinal's loud staccato call and find it perched at the top branches of a tall tree. From that day on the cardinal's calls become more frequent and persistent, it seems, in response to sunlight and warmth pooling on its red chest.

Place a photograph, print, or perhaps a figurine of a red cardinal on your altar. Illuminate it with a bank of candles.

Winter seems interminable. The snow is slushy and dirty during the day. At night the slush freezes into perilous patches of ice. The sun rarely shines and gloom settles over the spirit.

CHEERLESS MONTH

The world is gray and cheerless.
Winter lingers.
We feel chilled, oppressed.

A Place of Your Own

We dare not think
of Spring—
Not yet!
We make ourselves numb, insentient.

Rather than being
participants, artists, creators,
We endure
this cheerless month.

Yet there are subtle stirrings,
If only the faint
growing strength of the sun's light.

Surging, restless, creative
irresistible power of spring,
Awaken our dulled senses
and quicken our curiosity
That we might turn
our winter to spring.

This time of year challenges us—in a relatively benign way—to find a meaning in the midst of despair. Winter is an allegory for a despair that may visit us later in our lives. We won't find the meaning "out there"—in nature or through the help of another person. We must look within and find that part of us which, like nature in winter, is strong and, in an existential sense, invincible.

Albert Camus's words are unforgettable: "In the midst of winter I discovered in me an invincible summer."

Viktor Frankl, in recounting his experiences in a Nazi death camp, described desperate moments when he realized the freedom and power to find meaning even in the most horrible of circumstances. Once, hungry, frozen, on the brink of death, while numbly walking to a morning work detail, Frankl thought of his wife. Her presence became almost physical. The sun rose in a pale pink sky. Suddenly he realized something he'd never really grasped: the spiritual meaning of love—that salvation comes through love. At that improbable moment he knew fulfillment as never before. And he realized: No one, no set of circumstances, could deny him such a beautiful experience, if he willed it for himself. From such a realization in the midst of such a horrifying and almost hopeless situation, Frankl began to envision a school of psychotherapy he called *logotherapy*, that relied on each person's *will to meaning*.

Deep winter is a good time to test your ability to look inside yourself and find your sense of beauty and meaning and, especially, your indomitable will to meaning.

WITHIN ME, WAITING

If,
indeed,
I am part of all that I have met,
May I be mindful
during this gray, cheerless winter month

A Place of Your Own

That within me is the
spilling laughter of children
the spontaneous smile of a friend
greeting a friend,
the warm glow of being truly content,
at one and at peace with self and the Divine.

May I not forget,
the laughter, the smiles,
the human warmth,
Within me,
Ready to vanquish the gloom and depression
of this gray, cheerless month.

I find that the depths of winter provide a window—though etched with ice flowers—into the human condition.

THE HUMAN CONDITION

What does it mean
to be human?
What defines our condition?
Perhaps it is this:

We see beauty
In the midst of ugliness;

Edward Searl

Out of chaos
We create order;

In the depth of winter
We hope for spring;

When confronted by death
We choose Life.

Searching for Signs of Spring

Set your altar with many candles in imitation of the church's Candlemas—blessing of the candles. In a shallow earthen bowl or plate collect seeds you've gathered out of doors from dried stalks.

Groundhog Day is one of the sillier seasonal holidays, yet it always generates broad interest. Will a caged groundhog in Punxsutawney, Pennsylvania, sees its shadow on the morning of February 2? The folk legend contends that if the groundhog sees its shadow, the sun will scare it back into its hole and winter will last another six weeks. But should clouds block the sun, the groundhog stays above ground and spring will soon arrive.

February 2 is a *cross-quarter day*—halfway between the winter solstice and the spring equinox. The Christian celebration of Candlemas falls on this day. Their tradition was appropriated from a Roman custom of searching by candlelight outdoors, in early morning, for the harbingers of spring. Groundhog

Day also remembers a Celtic custom of lighting fires and sprinkling grain around those fires while chanting to the goddess of crops, "Bridget, come!"

Groundhog Day, as an oracle of spring, makes sense as a cross-quarter day. Winter, by the course of the sun and earth, is half over. We human beings, though, have had enough of winter. By general consensus, February is the dullest and dreariest month of the year.

Defy convention. Go out of doors on this February day and actively search for signs of spring: the call of birds, the swell of buds, the melting of ice and snow, the warmth of the sun, seeds on dry stalks, perhaps a crocus pushing itself above the ground by a sunny wall.

READING THE SIGNS

Even now
In the frozen depths of winter
Life beckons—
Holds a promise.
The sun rises a little earlier,
sets a little later each day;
Darkness diminishes.
And when the sun's rays touch
our faces,
We feel a returning warmth.

A Place of Your Own

Spring may hesitate—
winter strike again and harder—
lingering.
But spring will come.
We trust.
For the signs are sure,
The promise is real.

There is no denying winter its season.
We can only endure.
But even in its frozen depths,
Life beckons—
Holds a promise.

So it is for the many and varied seasons
of winter the human spirit endures.
Life beckons—
Holds a promise,
If only we read the signs
And trust.

While this devotion speaks of sacred love, that sacred love is realized in the material world. This altar honors Saint Valentine's Day. Use that day's customary symbols: candlelight, flowers—roses or carnations—the color red, even angelic messengers.

Mid-February brings us a holiday of love. It's often been said that *love* is one of the most overused and trivialized words, yet we *must* utter it again and again. This devotion explores the ideal of love born and reborn through human action.

Among our cultural values, love surely ranks highest. For many persons the source of that love is Divine, and Jesus is the great teacher of love in word and example.

A person who truly experiences it, internalizes this Divine Love and becomes a loving person: a simple and straightforward three part equation that Jesus, the Teacher, framed in response to a lawyer's cunning question.

Then one of them, which was a lawyer, asked him a question, tempting him, and saying, Master, which is the great commandment in the law? Jesus said unto him, Thou shalt love the Lord your God with all thy heart, and with all thy soul, and with all thy mind. This is the first and great commandment. And the second is like unto it, Thou shalt love thy neighbor as thyself. On these two commandments hang all the law and the prophets. (KJV, Matt. 22:36-40)

My universal religion draws from the Christian doctrine of love, especially Jesus of Nazareth's pronouncements and practices. I'm generally critical of the Apostle Paul, the apostle often credited as the architect of Christianity. Yet I believe that Paul's prose poem on love is a nearly perfect expression. I recognize, in Paul's words as in my own being, the insight of a person whose loving never quite reaches the perceived ideal and therefore is particularly full of passion.

If I speak in the tongues of men and of angels, but have not love, I am a noisy gong or clanging cymbal. And if I have prophetic powers, and understand all mysteries and all knowledge, and if I have all faith, so as to remove mountains, but have not love, I am nothing. . . .

Love is patient and kind, love is not jealous or boastful; it is not arrogant or rude. Love does not insist on its own way; it is not irritable or resentful; it does not rejoice in the right. Love bears all things, believes all things, hopes all things, endures all things.

Love never ends. . . .

So faith, hope, love abide, these three: But the greatest of these is Love. (RSV, I Cor. 13:1–13)

Thomas Kempis, in *Imitation of Christ*, echoed Paul's words and expanded upon what love is and does. Whenever I read this, it always tempts me to write my own litany of what love is, an exercise you might try to make this devotion on Divine Love your own.

Love is a great thing, a great good indeed, which alone makes light all that is burdensome, and bears with even mind all that is uneven. For it carries a burthen without being burthened; and it makes all that which is bitter sweet and savoury.

Nothing is sweeter than love; nothing stronger, nothing higher, nothing broader, nothing more pleasant, nothing fuller or better in heaven and in earth; for love is born of God, and can rest only in God above all things created.

Love often knows no measure, but warmly glows above all measure.

Love feels no burthen, regards not labours, would willingly do more than it is able, pleads not impossibility, because it feels sure that it can and may do all things. It is able, therefore, to do all things; and it makes good many deficiencies, and frees many things for being carried out, where he who loves, not faints and lies down.

Love watches, and sleeping slumbers not; weary, is not

tired; straightened, is not constrained; frightened, is not disturbed; but, like a living flame and a burning torch, it bursts forth upwards and safely overpasses all.

Love is swift, sincere, loyal, pleasant, and delightful; strong, patient, faithful, prudent, long-suffering, manly, and never seeking itself; for where a man seeks himself, there he falls from love.

Love is circumspect, humble, and upright; not weak, not fickle, not intent upon vain things; sober, chaste, steadfast, quiet, and guarded in all its senses.

The author of the John gospel wrote of the incredible power of human love.

No man hath seen God at any time. If we love one another, God dwelleth in us, and His love is perfected in us. (KJV, 1 John 4:12)

In this way, by the power of love in word and deed, we may become Creators of the highest order and bring the Divine into our world: ". . . love is perfected in us."

The Season of Lengthening Days

*Use this altar to display the bowl of tulips, daffo-
dils, narcissus, or paperwhites you've forced into
bloom. Keep this altar simple—spare and clean.*

A few years ago, as I approached full midlife,
I took a fifty-day sabbatical road trip
through the belly of America. I cast that
journey within the traditional forty days of Lent. I
began with Mardi Gras in New Orleans and ended
with Good Friday in Chimayo, New Mexico. I took
the time alone and designed a personally mythic journey to look deeply into myself, to make adjustments,
and to prepare myself for the second half of my life.
Lent provided the metaphor for this personal discipline. The midsection of America provided the setting—a continental altar.

Lent originally meant *spring* and came from an
Old English word meaning *lengthening days*. My soul
stirs as the days of midwinter become noticeably
longer, the sunlight seems stronger, and Nature gradually expands. I have a spring cleaning urge to restore, to generally make things right, and to prepare

my own soul. This happens every year. I come alive after a long
and dull lethargy.

LAWNS AND LENT

Sun and rain have melted
a winter's snow,
Revealing a season of litter:
pitted cinders and crumpled cans;
broken twigs and sodden papers;
shards of plastic and glass.

There they lay,
scattered and dirty,
Violating our spring need
for order, freshness, and beauty.

Similarly, you might discover
a season of litter deposited
on your spirit:
silent misgivings,
lethargy and laziness,
nagging guilts,
and perhaps secret sins.

Now is the time to make
things right,
To rake lawns

And, yes,
To purify your soul.

This is a time to ready yourself,
that you might be responsive to,
that you might be worthy of
The renewal and rebirth spring promises.

A wizened colleague, Clinton Lee Scott, whose Vermont roots made his writing spare and picturesque, alerted me to the truly human possibilities of Lent.

LENT

The Teutons of ancient days, after the long hard winter, re-joiced when the season's cold began to pass and the promise of spring was in the air. They held joyful festivals and sang praises to their gods. The "lengthening days" were for dancing and feasting.

Then the ponderous councils of the church moved in and proceeded to take the joy out of the season by prescribing that Lent be for self-denial, sackcloth and ashes, and a shortcut to holiness.

We should do better. Lent should be a season not of gloom, but of cheer, not sulfur and molasses but maple syrup and raised doughnuts, a time to celebrate the goodness, the beauty, and the utility in life.

Lent is a time not for monastic introspection but for ex-

pansion of mind and heart, for vigorous exercise and deep breathing, a time for getting the whole self tuned up so it can function harmoniously with the forces that lift the tulips and make the grass grow. It is a time for becoming more alive, for making love with your mate, and for getting acquainted with your children.

To use these weeks well, think in terms of relationships— how to deepen existing relationships and reestablish relationships that have dissipated. Think about your relationships in four dimensions:

1) with your essential self
2) with your fellow kind, especially your family and friends
3) with Nature
4) with the Divine.

Only you know what aspects of your relationships need emphasis. Maybe you need to connect with your own body through exercise. Maybe you need to reconcile with an estranged daughter or son. Maybe you need to deepen your commitment to your mate. Maybe you need to determine your connection with the Divinity of Life. Now is the time!

My cautionary counsel for all Lenten ventures involves preparation and patience.

Think of the Lenten discipline as the process of creating a garden, from the arrival of the seed catalog to the appearance of the first shoots. Let planning and planting guide you in your Lenten activities. That's what this season is all about—preparation and patience—because there is not only increasing hope but significant rewards throughout. No need to rush; no need to demand. But you must engage your imagination, exercise your will, and most of all do the work.

Week 10
Restoring a Personal Relationship

Focus this altar on the person or persons with whom you want to restore, repair, or fortify a relationship. Place on this altar a photograph of you with that person. Let it help you remember what you once had and what you've lost, or what you never had but which is possible now.

In traditional practice Lent means *penitence*—acts of denial and discipline to atone for sins. *Atonement* is one of those words that unfolds its own meaning when you examine its components. *Atonement=at+one+ment.* It is to be *at one*—of one mind, in accord, in relationship. We've grown accustomed to thinking of atonement as a process of purification involving penance. But that's only one means to the goal of a right relationship and apt to miss the mark. Why not deal directly with your relationships?

Through genuine relationships we find the most satisfying meanings possible. In a perfect relationship, we exist, if only for a moment, in mystical bliss. We are alive and also saved. The Divine comes into fuller being through the relationship.

Natural rhythms of Nature and self make this a good season to seek at-one-ment in your relationships. Begin with a searching question.

HOLDING BACK

I know
Your feelings
of aloneness, of isolation,
of separation
As well as
you know mine.

In our yearnings
for companionship,
for connection,
for love,
for union,
We are the same.

Why is it then,
Between you and me
There is a holding back
of one's self from the other?

What are we saving ourselves from,
or for,
Anyway?

Utter a simple prayer that you may dare to make, restore, or deepen a relationship, rich in possibilities, yet unfulfilled.

THREE GIFTS

The grace to love myself,
The vision to love my fellow kind,
The courage to leap across
the abyss of our separateness
And risk loving you
without regard for rejection or gain,
Spirit of Love,
Bless me,
Bless us
With these three gifts.

Once again we come to love. Love encompasses the rich possibilities of human relationships. It creates relationships, and it is the fulfillment of relationships. It points to God and brings God into being.

POWER OF OUR LOVE

If there is Divinity
within each of us,
There is a grace
We can bestow upon one another.
It comes through

concern, compassion,
interest, involvement,
an easiness of giving and receiving.
It is, most simply, love.
Through love
we create one another
and ourselves.
Love is the most potent force
in the universe.
Through it and in it
We are creators of the highest order.
We are gods who ache
to quicken, inspire,
nurture, and sustain—
bringing happiness and peace.

Know the Divinity within,
the grace and the power of your love.

Between Winter and Spring

Fill a small flower pot with soil and plant in it a few seeds. The kind of seed, flower or vegetable, really doesn't matter. On your altar this planted pot represents the life, dormant and hidden, that waits for winter to melt into spring.

The most difficult time of year for me is this in-between time. I want to leap from winter directly to spring. I worry if another bout of cold weather will damage new buds and new growth. When it does happen I take it personally. I urge myself to remain patient and to trust—accepting and appreciating these in-between days. But I don't want to lose a reasonable and wonderful expectation—the hope of spring. I take stock and make a resolution to appreciate and live fully even in these difficult days between winter and spring.

BETWEEN

Between . . .
Between winter and spring.

E d w a r d   S e a r l

One day sparkling rivulets
rush into the gutters.
The next day the rivulets
freeze into white snakes.
One day brown matted grass appears
among hillocks of gray and dirty
snow.
The next day a clean white blanket
once again covers all.

In the last days of winter
we know what it means
to be between:
Between what has been
and what will be.

Sometimes it is difficult
to live in the present,
—in the here and now—
When it is between.
We have grown wary and anxious.
We search the signs of change.
We rejoice in the harbingers:
returning robins and swelling buds
and longer evenings.

Surely we need the hope of spring
erasing winter.

> *But we also need the courage and wisdom*
> *to use the days which are between . . .*
> *Days such as today,*
> *Between . . .*

> *Between winter and spring.*

When I let my inner spirit find its reflection in Nature in these in-between days, I realize my life seesaws between despair and hope. This is a hard realization, but an important one.

RELUCTANT WINTER/HESITANT SPRING

> *The dull brown of the earth,*
> *now the snow has melted*
> *but spring hasn't worked its miracles,*
> *May make you sad.*
> *That's all right. Don't resist the sadness.*
> *Feel it. Know the sadness—*
> *know from where it comes.*
> *The sadness will pass,*
> *if you confront it*
> *and give it its time.*
> *It will be good to remember*
> *in the sun-warmed days to come*
> *That there is sadness there too,*
> *waiting its day.*

And know
in the sadness you now feel
There is also joy
waiting its season.

Now, in these in-between days
of reluctant winter and hesitant spring
There is a sense of Life and living's
Roundness,
As there is always and everywhere
a sense of Life and living's
Roundness,
If only we can see it.

I have a personal visualization that helps me find patience
and strength. I imagine my weary and anxious spirit as a seed.

WAITING

Waiting.
Beneath the snow.
In cold ground.
Waiting.
The patient seed
bides its time.
Waiting
for spring sun.
Waiting for spring rain.

A Place of Your Own

Waiting out
gray skies and frigid winds.
Beneath the snow.
In its hard husk.
Waiting. The seed:
A kernel of life.
Waiting for its Season.

The human heart
is a seed.
Waiting. The heart:
In its hard husk.
In its cold round.
Through its winter.
Biding its time.
Patient.
Waiting for its springtime.

Mover of the Seasons,
Bring that springtime
to winter hearts.

An open door provides an apt symbol for this devotion. Find such a photograph or print to put on this altar to help you meditate upon the risk and rewards of crossing thresholds. What is a door, but an opening in an arbitrary construction that confines space?

Certain threshold situations make me uncertain and sometimes cowardly. I persuade myself that I prefer the familiar even though I find it dreary or know it has drawn to its inevitable ending. When I walk over the threshold, when I make the transition, I know I'm going to have to adjust, adapt, and risk possible failure.

As wonderful as I know spring will be, a little piece of me wants to stay in what has become the *undemanding* winter.

SPRING *IS* A DANGEROUS TIME

Teased by the sun's waxing warmth,
Forsythia buds ache to bloom,
Yet Winter seeps down
from the north,

> *And the temperature plummets.*
> *And snow falls.*
> *And swollen buds are vulnerable.*
> *Will they freeze? We wonder.*
>
> *There is always risk*
> *in living, responding, opening—loving.*
> *Winter,*
> *in human guise,*
> *Can sear and destroy.*
>
> *Spring is a dangerous time.*
> *And no one can foresee*
> *the consequences.*
> *But the alternative for us,*
> *Never to risk a springtide*
> *of the spirit*
> *Has the surest of consequences:*
> *It will always be winter in our hearts.*

My mentor Ralph Waldo Emerson always reminds me that I have no choice but to accept change—that is Creation's design.

FROM WOODNOTES

> *All the forms are fugitive,*
> *But the substances survive,*

Ever fresh the broad Creation,
A Divine improvisation,
From the heart of God proceeds,
A single will, a million deeds.

I find it helps me to affirm that, while creation is forever new, what was will endure—and not just in memory. The old gives birth to the new; the new forever gives the old a new life. I realize that *change* is really the only *continuity* there can be.

ALWAYS A BEGINNING

Always there is a beginning—
a new day,
a new month,
a new season,
a new year.
Forever the old passes away
and newness emerges
from the richness that was.
Nothing is ever lost
in the many changes
time brings.
What was,
in some way,
Will be,
though changed in form.

A Place of Your Own

>Rejoice in beginnings
>in the heritage from which they emerge,
>in the freshness which they bring,
>in the hope which they offer,
>in the promise they hold.

>Know this:
>This moment is a beginning,
>And Life
>Is full of richness,
>of freshness,
>of hope,
>and of promise.

Small statues of St. Francis are quite common, sometimes with small birds to which, it is said, he once preached. I adorn my altar with a photograph of bird shadows projected on the courtyard wall of a New Mexico bed and breakfast where I stayed one Holy Week. The birds were attracted by seeds strewn around a statue of St. Francis.

Any array of objects from or representing Nature can set your altar, dedicated not to St. Francis, but to the spirit of his life and the gentle love of Life he taught.

I n my estimation, Francis of Assisi was a genuine saint. Francis brought renewed spirituality and piety to a church that by 1200 had reached its pinnacle of worldliness. Francis wasn't complicated. He lived in humility and in poverty. When the first religious order he founded became too large and unwieldy to control, Francis gave up its leadership.

Francis took his personal piety out into the world. His famous prayer is a plan of action for those who know Divine love. It's a good prayer for anytime of the year, but even more appropriate as we venture into the new creation of spring.

> *Lord, make me an instrument of thy peace.*
> *Where there is hatred, let me sow love;*
> *Where there is injury, pardon;*
> *Where there is doubt, faith;*
> *Where there is despair, hope;*
> *Where there is darkness, light; and*
> *Where there is sadness, joy.*

> *Divine Master,*
> *Grant that I may not so much seek to be*
> *Consoled as to console;*
> *To be understood as to understand;*
> *To be loved as to love;*
> *For it is in giving that we receive;*
> *It is in pardoning that we are pardoned;*
> *And it is in dying that we are born*
> *to eternal life.*

Francis combined two practical and great loves—of humankind and of Nature. Familiar garden statuary represents Francis preaching to the sparrows—I imagine the sparrows were preaching to him, too. He introduced the creche to the observance of Christmas, and for eight centuries animals have had a close association with the beauty of the Nativity story.

On the brink of spring, all Creation—inanimate Nature,

Edward Searl

plants and trees, birds and animals, human beings, too—lift a joyous hymn to the glorious source of wonderful Creation.

All Creatures of the Earth and Sky,
Come, kindred, lift your voices high,
Alleluia, Alleluia!
Bright burning sun with golden beam,
Soft shining moon with silver gleam:
Alleluia, Alleluia, Alleluia, Alleluia, Alleluia!

Swift rushing wind so wild and strong,
White clouds that sail in heav'n along,
Alleluia, Alleluia!
Fair rising morn in praise rejoice,
High stars of evening find a voice:
Alleluia, Alleluia, Alleluia, Alleluia, Alleluia!

Cool flowing water, pure and clear,
Make music for all life to hear,
Alleluia, Alleluia!
Dance, flame of firs so strong and bright,
And bless us with your warmth and light:
Alleluia, Alleluia, Alleluia, Alleluia, Alleluia!

Embracing earth, you, day by day,
Bring forth your blessing on our way,
Alleluia, Alleluia!

All herbs and fruits that richly grow
Let them the glory also show:
Alleluia, Alleluia, Alleluia, Alleluia, Alleluia!

All you of understanding heart,
Forgiving others, take your part,
Alleluia, Alleluia!
Let all things now the Holy bless,
And worship God in humbleness:
Alleluia, Alleluia, Alleluia, Alleluia, Alleluia!
[attributed to St. Francis]

spring

In creating your spring altar use things that represent what spring brings and means to you. I seek out heavily budded forsythia branches and arrange them in a clear glass vase. I love their simplicity and the arrangement will last for days. I light two frosted-glass votives and place them on either side of the vase. Their warm glow reminds me of spring light.

For me, spring doesn't depend on the calendar. Unmistakable sensations tell me that winter, though it may not be over, is losing its hold. My senses waken from a winter lethargy. I'm attentive to signs of change, no matter how subtle.

I'm inspired and stirred to action. An urge to clean, tune, and spruce up rises in me—perhaps a vestige of an ancient nesting instinct.

Spring involves renewal, but even more miraculously restores hope—an early gift of this season. I am joyful.

SPRING BEGINS

Spring begins
At that precise winter's moment
(Be it December or March),
When the senses—
Aroused by the trickle
of melting snow
or
warmth of the waxing sun—
Leap in sudden expectation
And despair is transformed
Into hope.

For weeks, I've created altars set with harbingers of spring—symbolic seeds to be planted and daffodil bulbs forced to bloom indoors. I've imagined the approaching balance of night and day and have sought a similar balance in my own being. Now, the vernal equinox that marks spring on the calendar calls for a special altar. It seems right to set this altar simply, with a clear glass vase of budded branches, which will open over the coming week. What causes those buds to swell works in me, too.

SAP RISING AND EMOTIONS FLOWING

Who is not moved
by the longer days,
the stronger, warmer sunlight,

> the clearer skies
> the singing birds?
>
> Who does not feel
> emotions flowing
> with sap rising in the trees?
>
> Why question
> the how or why it is so.
> There are other times
> better suited for inquiry—
> perhaps the depths of dark winter nights.
>
> For now,
> Isn't it enough
> just to see, to feel, to know
> winter has turned to spring?
>
> So, for now,
> simply experience.
> Rejoice deeply.
> And pray
> the power of the cycling seasons
> will thaw every wintry heart.

As the waxing sun gradually transforms Nature, a long gentleness settles upon my soul. I'm satisfied. I wish I could stop time.

The uncomplicated beauty of my spring altar reminds me to keep a simple, hopeful attitude. The opening of the buds teaches me patience.

EARLY SPRING

This is the season—
Spring—
of dormant Life reviving,
and recreation through birth.
This is a time
to be quiet and still—
Not to shut out primary experience
by multiplying words and activity.
This is a time
to be empty and to be receptive,
That you might feel
deep in your being
Life's irresistible upward urge—
Becoming one with that Life
And becoming new again,
Yourself.

Be quiet.
Be still.
Be empty.
Be receptive.
Be one

With patient, swelling Life.
And in time you
Will be revived and renewed,
too,
One with Life in spring.

    As days advance and the branches on my spring altar blossom into bright yellow flowers and unfurl green leaves, the season progresses toward what poet James Russell Lowell called the "high tide of the year." Advancing spring can make me giddy. I wish a little giddiness for you.

GRACE OF SPRING

Grace of spring,
Inflate heavy hearts
with helium;
Paint grayness
in pastels
and astonishing whites;
Fill ears
with the call of birds
and whisper of tender leaves;
Make aching feet youthful
to romp and dance
on moist earth.

Grace of spring,
Continue to
Renew youth,
Stir hope,
Cleanse senses,
And lift spirits
In this most wondrous of seasons.

In the midst of spring, I marvel at the alchemy that transforms nature and soul. I identify with the person Emerson once noted in his journal: "I have just seen a man who told me that his eyes opened as he grew older, and that every spring was more beautiful to him than the last."

When I wake to a dawn splendor that stirs my soul or when I anticipate an auspicious day, I set my altar with a favorite photograph I've taken. My choice varies according to the season: dewdrop jewels on meadow grass in spring or summer, the sun rising beyond brightly colored autumn trees, or fresh snow, sculpted and glistening after a winter storm. I light a votive in a faceted glass holder. The facets sparkle with the flame.

How do you begin your day? Do you sleep until the last possible moment and, still half asleep, stumble to the kitchen to make breakfast for your family? Do you rush to get ready for work? Do you turn on the television or radio to a hectically paced program of awful news reports and loud commercials, as you read the paper, and gulp your breakfast?

A jumbled morning is a melancholy beginning to a day. Take control and set a positive tone that will stay with you for hours. Begin your day with a blessing. Give just a few minutes of attention to your altar and focus your intentions when you wake. Commit to an agreeable attitude that will encourage you to meet whatever the day demands of you.

Nancy Eberle, one of six contemporary working women who collaborated in the book *Reinventing Home*, wrote of the importance of attending to the day's first moments:

> *The key to morning time well spent is any activity that allows you to—in the words of the gurus—"be here now." Or more simply put, to pay attention. The wonderful thing about such time is that you get double your money. The peacefulness you experience during morning hours is there to come back to again at any time throughout the day, whereas it is nearly impossible to find once you have hurtled from bed to full involvement. So what we are talking about is consciousness, being conscious of who you are and where you are before (I am tempted to say before all hell breaks loose)—before the day with all its demands gets the jump on you.*

Your altar can invoke a morning peace, even though you've already set it for another occasion. Simply preface your devotions with a poem attributed to a third century Hindu poet, Kalidasa.

THE EXHORTATION TO THE DAWN

Look to this day!
For it is life, the very life of life.

A Place of Your Own

> *In its brief course lie all the verities*
> *and realities of your existence:*
> *The bliss of growth,*
> *The glory of action,*
> *The splendor of beauty;*
> *For yesterday is but a dream,*
> *And tomorrow is only a vision;*
> *But today, well lived, makes every*
> *yesterday*
> *A dream of happiness*
> *And every tomorrow a vision of*
> *hope.*
> *Look well, therefore, to this day.*

Certain mornings are brilliant, and I am full of enthusiasm.

A NEW CREATION

> *There are days, oh, what days*
> *when the air is clear*
> *and the sun is strong,*
> *Days when I am most alive!*

> *My senses are heightened,*
> *made more acute,*
> *As though I've awakened*
> *to a new creation.*

And I am a new creature
exploring a new earth.

I'm astonished by the roundness
of the domed sky.

Has it ever been such a delicate shade
of curving blue?
Will it ever be again?

I pause to feel the sunny, airy ether
flow around me.

I breathe deep draughts of the fresh air.
I purify and refresh my soul.
Yes, I feel my soul surging within me.

From the outlines of trees
against the embracing sky
To the folding contours of the earth,
All things between sky and ground
are captured in the purest, clearest crystal.

For a lingering, precious moment
Nature and I are suspended
in the wonder of time and space.

A Place of Your Own

> *There are days, oh, what days*
> *when the air is clear*
> *and the sun is strong,*
> *Days such as today*
> *When I awaken to a new creation!*

Such a glory enlivens me. I claim the day. Confident, I step into the promises and possibilities.

*For this devotion I use a single flower. I give spe-
cial attention to its display. My favorite presentation is
to float the flower head in a shallow, clear glass bowl.
The floating flower has a transcendental quality.*

My professional life turns on crafting and
presenting weekly sermons. After twenty
years of sermonizing, I've acquired a
practical sense of what works. Tangible examples
drawn from real, human experiences have a greater
effect than abstractions of philosophy and theology.

In my estimation the most eloquent sermon ever
given had no words. There are several versions of that
sermon but only one haunting image: the Buddha
standing in front of his disciples, a golden lotus in
his hands. A single flower: simple, confrontational,
and experiential. Nothing could have been more perfect. The body language of the disciples was clear.
No one understood the meaning of this sermon except Mahakasyapa who had a quiet smile on his face.
This register of understanding caused the Buddha to
designate Mahakasyapa his successor. Passing from

Mahakasyapa through the twenty-eight patriarchs in India and carried to China in 520 by Bodhidharma, this tradition migrated to Japan in the twelfth century and became the religion of Zen Buddhism.

The Buddha, in forgoing words, offered his followers, and the generations to follow, a persuasive object lesson in the living experience of religion—that *it* was not his to give but the disciple's to grasp, just as the Buddha himself had grasped *it*. *It* is always beyond the ability of words to express.

In Zen, this immediate grasping of meaning is *satori*—the equivalent of what in the West we call a mystical experience and its intuitive knowledge—that comes through a process of seated meditation know as *zazen*. The Buddha's famous flower sermon insinuates the possibilities of a personal altar set with simple, yet evocative things—things that focus intuitive understandings.

The Buddha's choice of a golden lotus was intentional. Flowers are recurring symbols in spiritual speculation and have the means to awaken intuitive understandings.

> *To see the world in a grain of*
> *sand,*
> *And heaven in a wild flower;*
> *Hold infinity in the palm of your*
> *hand,*
> *And eternity in an hour.*
> —*William Blake*, Auguries of Innocence

Jesus advised in his own eloquent sermon, the Sermon on the Mount:

Consider the lilies of the field, how they grow; they toil not neither do they spin: And yet I say unto you, That even Solomon in all his glory was not arrayed like one of these. (KJV, Matt. 6:28–29)

Alfred Lord Tennyson poeticized:

> *Flower in the crannied wall,*
> *I pluck you out of the crannies—*
> *Hold you here, root and all, in my hand,*
> *Little flower—but if I could understand*
> *What you are, root and all, and all in all,*
> *I should know what God and man is.*

With no further instruction, place a single flower on your altar and sit in quiet meditation before it. I prefer to do this in early afternoon, my altar bathed in bright sunlight pouring in through a nearby window. Spring, the season of flowers, is particularly well suited for this devotion. Repeat this flower altar and meditation, from early spring's first bloom through autumn's final flower.

Insight and understanding might come suddenly and you get *it*. *It* might also take a long time to occur. Or *it* might not occur at all. That's all right, too. Be patient, assured that the process—quiet meditation—is as significant as the outcome.

The beauty of a flower has a meaning that needs no elaboration. To appreciate the beauty is a spiritual act.

I snip a picturesque maple branch engorged with reddish buds, and arrange it in imitation of Japanese simplicity in an earthen vase. I light tall tapers on either side of the branches so the buds will absorb the glow and warmth of the flames.

At other times of the year a photograph of a night sky with a single, early star serves as a reminder of the child's admonishment: "You be glad at that star!"

If you're too self-absorbed, you can miss the subtle growth of early spring. This happened to me not long ago. I was overworked and unhappy, restless and constrained by circumstances. Nature's changes passed by virtually unnoticed. But I remember as though it were yesterday the exact moment my eyes opened. I was amazed. I admonished myself to practice what I preach—to pay attention to the graces and gifts Life presents in every moment.

ASTONISHED!

Anxious. Expectant.
I wished
the signs of spring
And felt disappointment
That winter lingered.
So hard. So long.

Yesterday. Looking
out a window
while it rained,
I saw
Engorged buds of a maple
opening.

Astonished! Chastised!
Why was I so surprised?
So uplifted? So ashamed
at my ability to look
and not see?
To live
— and not be alive?

This memory explains why I wait for maple trees to come
into full-leaf bud for this devotion. I reflect upon my awareness
as my gaze appreciates the maple branch I've arranged on my
altar.

A colleague in the ministry, Clarke Dewey Wells, tells a classic story about petty enemies of the spirit. Whenever I read it, I consider the poetic truth of the biblical prophesy found in KJV, Isaiah 11: 6—"a little child shall lead them."

YOU BE GLAD AT THAT STAR

Several years ago and shortly after twilight, our 3½-year-old tried to direct his parents' attention to a shining star.

The parents were busy with time and schedules, the irritabilities of the day and other worthy preoccupations. "Yes, yes, we see the star—now I'm busy, don't bother me." On hearing this the young one launched through the porch door, fixed us with a fiery gaze and said, "You be glad at that star!"

I will not forget the incident or his perfect words. It was one of the rare moments when you get everything you need for the good of your soul—reprimand, disclosure and blessing. It was especially good for me, that surprising moment, because I am one who responds automatically and negatively to the usual exhortations to pause-and-be-more-appreciative-of-life-unquote. Fortunately, I was caught grandly off-guard.

There is a notion, with some truth in it, that we cannot command joy, happiness, appreciation, fulfillment. We do not engineer the seasons of the soul or enjoin the quality of mood in another; and yet, I do believe there is right and wisdom in that imperative declaration—you be glad at that star!

If we cannot impel ourselves into stellar gladness, we

can at least clean the dust from the lens of our perception; if we cannot dictate our own fulfillment, we can at least steer in the right direction; if we cannot exact a guarantee for a more appreciative awareness of our world—for persons and stars and breathing and tastes and the incalculable gift of every day—we can at least prescribe some of the conditions through which an increased awareness is more likely to open up the skies, for us and for our children.

It is not always the great evils that obstruct and waylay our joy. It is our unnecessary and undignified surrender to the petty enemies—and I suggest it is our duty to scheme against them and make them subservient to human decree: time, schedules, our irritabilities of the day, and other worthy preoccupations. Matters more subtle and humane should command our lives. You be glad at that star.

It's inevitable. We all lose innocence and wonder to some degree. When that happens, we die a little. These little deaths add up. I'm indebted to another colleague, Max Coots, for an affirmation that helps me choose life over death.

FROM Seasons of the Self

It's the little deaths before the final time we fear.
The blasé shrug that quietly replaces excited curiosity,
The cynic-sneer that takes the place of innocence,
The soft-sweet odor of success that overcomes the sense of
    sympathy.

A Place of Your Own

The self-betrayals that rob us of our will to trust,
The ridicule of vision, the barren blindness to what was
  once our sense of beauty—
These are deaths that come so quietly we do not know when
  it was we died.

The eggshell of a songbird you may have found earlier this spring is the perfect setting for this Easter altar. In addition, or instead, begin this devotion with a small basket of hens' eggs. At the completion of the devotion, boil the eggs, then decorate them with the abandon and joy of your childhood. Keep these decorated eggs on your altar throughout the week as a reminder of Life's fertile gifts.

It was early spring. I'd planted bulbs in the autumn and was looking for signs of their growth beneath a big pine in front of my house. Poking among damp leaves, I found a broken bird's egg. It was small and an astonishing blue. A dab of yellow yolk clung to the utter whiteness of the inner surface. The broken shell felt especially fragile to fingers that were a little clumsy in the chilly air.

I removed my glasses to give it a closer look. Memories flooded from my childhood. In my memory's eye I saw similar eggs I'd found in long ago springtimes now unexpectedly resurrected. They were mostly robins' eggs, usually fragments like the broken shell in my hand.

When I was a kid, those shells, flecked with a little dried blood or yolk, scared me. Those shells gave me an early and direct encounter with life and death—a reality so fragile that I didn't dare hold it in my hands. To be truthful, I'm still squeamish. Life is not easy to face—not in its full realities, because the realities are ambiguous.

I sometimes speculate that my deepest, most secret motive for becoming a minister was in reaction to this squeamishness. My liberal tradition encourages me to face Life liberally, squarely, honestly, and realistically—summarized as "to speak the truth in love." My profession brings me face-to-face with the mortality of persons I respect and love.

The day I found the eggshell, I'd been thinking about my usual Easter dilemma, to fashion for Easter Sunday remarks that would bring together the rich complexity of ancient myths and celebrations of the spring equinox, Jewish Passover, and Christian Easter. For me drawing these traditions together isn't a matter of political correctness. I'm a universalist, a humanist, a naturalistic mystic. I appreciate an underlying unity in Easter's complexities. I'm passionate about timeless human religious experience. The eggshell in my hand sent me thinking about the egg's varied symbolism.

For a moment I envied the Buddha, who preached a sermon to his disciples by silently holding a flower in his hands; yet only one disciple "got *it*." I knew I'd get a worse response if I stood silently for twenty minutes in front of my congregation with this eggshell in my cupped hands. It was, however, perfect for my private altar.

Placed on a bed of dried leaves, the eggshell evokes the mysteries and realities of the season. A similar shell you've found and arranged might be just the thing to set on your altar this Easter.

It's not by chance that so many traditions have adopted the symbolism of the egg. Draw on that symbolism to honor your faith tradition or to explore a universal meaning. Set your Easter altar with a basket of eggs. For your devotion consider how various traditions have given the egg symbolic meaning.

Christians see a chick hatching as a reminder of Jesus breaking out of the tomb and are drawn into the complex mystery of the Resurrection.

Jews place a roasted egg on the Passover Seder plate to represent fertility, renewal, and rebirth. The egg helps to remind them of ancient covenants made with God, renewed by each generation.

Hindus envision an ancient creation story in which the World Egg broke in two, hatching the sun. One half of the shell created a golden sky, the other half a silver earth. The waters of the earth sprung from the layers just under the shell.

Modern pagans draw upon remnants of ancient Celtic and Druid ceremonies performed in sacred groves. In one ceremony Druids formed a circle around a pile of serpent eggs—the eggs represented Life and the circle of worshipers enacted its endless chain.

Beyond all these representations, the egg stands for the female—the life giver. Its roundness is feminine. In higher forms of life, the egg, when fertilized, creates new life. It symbolizes the Goddess that was the earliest personification of the Divine.

The egg is a religious symbol more ancient and universal than the cross and still youthful enough to create new customs. I'm thinking of the relatively recent growing custom of decorating bare branched trees with eggs—Easter trees like Christmas trees, yet another variation on the tree of life motif. For me, Easter is an expansive expression of human religion.

Be playful with this altar dedicated to the diversity of Life and the interdependent web of Creation. Perhaps you have small animal figurines you can arrange with bits of wood, moss, rocks, or other found objects from Nature. I use a small print of a primitive "Peacable Kingdom" painting in which a lion sleeps with a lamb, inspired by the familiar passage from Isaiah.

In midspring, I feel a kindredness to all living things. I'm alive, my senses keen. The grass is green, leaves are full, flowers and shrubs are blooming, bees are buzzing, and birds are singing. I celebrate how precious my life is and, by empathy, how precious all Life is.

A favorite expression of this kindredness comes from the passionate writing of Alan Devoe, a mid-century naturalist.

FROM LIVES AROUND US

The life of earth is all of a piece. For all of us, whether men or toads or meadow-mice or towering trees, there is birth and a life-adventure and ultimately a death; we are all a part of the same tremendous rhythms and rituals, all fragments of similar destiny, all travelers through the same inscrutable experience toward an inexplicable bourne. Our human blood partakes, so to speak, of fox-blood; our human song differs not signally from the song of orioles; in us are a-stir the impulses that stir not greatly differently in an oak or a stone or a cabbage-butterfly or a constellation.

With this strong awareness in the front of my consciousness, I set my altar with the small print of a Peaceable Kingdom painting that depicts a lion and lamb and other animals dwelling together in harmony. While this would never occur in Nature, I see this as a projection we humans can make on a spiritual plane—that all Life is connected and kindred.

Creation is marvelous. It seems to testify to a Creator and a Divine love.

"The universe, high and wide and deep, is but a handful of God-enchanted dust," Theodore Parker rhapsodized a century and a half ago.

"Do not be vexed at your delight in creatures and things. But do not let it shackle itself to creatures and things; through these, press on to God," Martin Buber recommended in the first half of the twentieth century.

Cecil Alexander poeticized, in the mid-nineteenth century:

> *All things bright and beautiful,*
> *All creatures great and small,*

All things wise and wonderful,
The Lord God made them all.

Always my reflection on Divine love returns my thoughts to
Nature and the preciousness of all Life forms. It's not enough
to merely reflect on this. Right thoughts must become right
actions. I must live the ethic that Albert Schweitzer called "reverence for Life."

A Buddhist blessing I reworked from the famous Metta
Sutta, becomes a personal vow to cultivate boundless goodwill.

Happiness and serenity to all beings!
Joy to you! May you be safe and free from fear.
Whatever your condition—
weak or strong, small or great,
invisible or visible, close at hand or far away,
already born or to be born someday,
In whatever realm of existence—
primeval or highly evolved,
undistinguished or esteemed,
unknown or known,
Be totally content and at ease.

Do not deceive another being:
let your actions be guileless.

Do not despise any being for any reason:
let your intentions be benign.

A Place of Your Own

Do not even wish, especially in anger or irritation,
that another being might suffer:
let your thoughts be compassionate.

As a parent cherishes an only child,
cherish all beings with total mindfulness
and an all encompassing heart.

Goodwill, then, to all beings—
you and you and you without limit—
radiating in all directions to include
the whole world without exception.

Mindfulness and the Moment

In preparing this altar think of something that you see or do everyday and take for granted. It could be a handful of dirt, a magazine, a photograph of a person with whom you live or work, leaves from a tree. . . . Place that item, or its representation, on your altar. Keep it simple—just one thing. Its very ordinariness will help you grasp the miracle of mindfulness, a spiritual state of mind that reveals that the so-called ordinary is extraordinary.

There are days when I feel in complete balance with Life. I'm not without an identity, but I'm not egocentric. Such a day becomes a doorway opening to true and full being.

Deep spring, surrounded with young life in every aspect of Nature, is particularly suited for bringing on this essential religious experience. Maybe this time of year stirs memories of my young consciousness—the personal Garden of Eden I left when my childhood ended—that existed before I became self-absorbed and ego laden.

Emerson spoke of the experience of total relationship in *Nature*.

Standing on the bare ground—my head bathed by the blithe air, and uplifted into infinite space—all mean egotism vanishes. I become a transparent eye-ball. I am nothing. I see all. The currents of Universal Being circulate through me; I am part or particle of God.

The image of the transparent eyeball makes me laugh, because I sense how much Emerson strained to convey the transcendental experience.

I think this is what Thich Nhat Hanh, a Vietnamese Buddhist monk, means by *mindfulness*. The spiritual discipline of mindfulness speaks to many of us whose lives are busy with unfulfilling activities and whose minds are filled to overflowing with distractions.

THE MIRACLE OF MINDFULNESS

Mindfulness is the miracle by which we master and restore ourselves. . . . Mindfulness is like that—it is the miracle which can call back in a flash our dispersed mind and restore it to wholeness so that we can live each minute of life. . . .

I like to walk alone on country paths, rich plants and wild grasses on both sides, putting each foot down on the earth in mindfulness, knowing that I walk on the wondrous earth. In such moments, existence is a miraculous and mysterious reality. People usually consider walking on water or in thin air a miracle. But I think the real miracle is not to walk either on water or in thin air, but to walk on earth.

Every day we are engaged in a miracle which we don't even recognize: a blue sky, white clouds, green leaves, the black, curious eyes of a child—our own two eyes. All is a miracle.

Walt Whitman was a natural prophet of mindfulness and the moment.

There was never any more inception than there is now,
Nor any more youth or age than there is now,
And will never be any more perfection than there is now,
Nor any more heaven or hell than there is now.

Will you seek afar off? you surely come back at last,
In things best known to you finding the best,
In persons nearest to you finding the sweetest, strongest,
  lovingest.
Happiness, knowledge, not in another place but this place,
not for another hour but this hour.

Mindfulness embeds you in the reality of the moment and gives you whatever that moment holds for you. Mindfulness reveals the holiness of every moment.

THIS MOMENT

It is no accident,
this moment we share.
In this moment
is all the time there ever was.

> *In this moment*
> *is all the time ever will be.*
>
> *As the moment burst out of the past,*
> *so it always gives way*
> *to the future rushing toward it.*
>
> *In this moment is eternity—*
> *yet fleeting, ephemeral,*
> *always acquiring, changing, becoming,*
> *so that it cannot be grasped.*
>
> *It is no accident,*
> *this moment we share.*
> *In this moment*
> *is all the time there ever was.*
> *In this moment*
> *is all the time ever will be.*
>
> *This moment is holy,*
> *as eternity is holy,*
> *as all moments are holy.*

This devotion gives me reserves upon which to draw throughout the year. Because of the unique qualities of the season, this nearly perfect day is rich in realizations—realizations I don't want to forget. Today I follow Emerson's counsel: "Write it on your heart that every day is the best day in the year."

Celebrate Mother-Spirit with a photograph and mementos of your mother, perhaps something she made. Mothers, include photographs and mementos of your children. Fathers, include photographs of your wife and children. I add a tumbled beach stone that resembles a mother curled around a child. You might add a similar representation or symbol of the Universal Mother or the Goddess, including Mary. And of course, add a traditional Mother's Day offering, a bouquet of flowers.

I remember the exact moment I realized the Life my Mother had given me.

My daughter Katy was nine months old and experiencing her first spring. My mother carried Katy crooked in her arm so Katy's face was level with hers. Together they explored the yard. Mom stopped in front of a patch of bright tulips. Her voice was at an excited pitch. "Look, Katy!" My daughter's gaze settled on the red flowers. "What's

that?" Mom intoned. Katy had the preverbal, total body response that indicated she understood and wanted to please.
Her eyes were big and full. "What is it?" Mom repeated, adding curiosity to her inflection. Then Mom carefully said, "It's
. . . a . . . flower!" After a pause, she added, "Isn't it beautiful?"

Mom continued the sequence from patch of flower to
patch of flower. "Look! What's that? It's a flower. Isn't it beautiful?"

That's how I was introduced to the world with a Mother's
kind of love that lives throughout a lifetime. That's how I
acquired curiosity, a sense of beauty, and love for Nature. I
can see how that love gave me connection, at-homeness,
knowledge, a sure sense of self, and even freedom. It gave me
the means to make and have my own life.

My wife, Ellie, gave our daughter, Katy, a variation of
this empowering love. I've no doubt that Katy will give it to
her children. From mother to daughter through the generations.

A friend gave me the small beach stone, a piece of natural,
found art, that looks like a mother curved around her child. For
me it represents the Universal Mother, the Goddess whose
month from Roman times has been May. I place that stone,
along with a photograph of my mom and my wife, Ellie, the
mother of my child, on my Mother's Day altar with, of course,
a flower bouquet.

Every time I reflect on this special Mother's love and how it made me who I am, I appreciate even more this Walt Whitman poem.

> Unfolded out of the folds of the woman man comes
> unfolded, and is always to come unfolded,
> Unfolded only out of the superbest woman of the earth is to
> come the superbest man of the earth,
> Unfolded out of the friendliest woman is to come the
> friendliest man,
> Unfolded only out of the perfect body of a woman can a
> man be form'd of perfect body,
> Unfolded only out of the inimitable poems of woman can
> come the poems of man, (only thence have my poems
> come;)
> Unfolded out of the strong and arrogant woman I love, only
> thence can appear the strong and arrogant man I love
> Unfolded by brawny embraces from the well-muscled
> woman I love, only thence come the brawny embraces of
> the man.
> Unfolded out of the folds of the woman's brain come all the
> folds of the man's brain, duly obedient,
> Unfolded out of the justice of the woman all justice is
> unfolded,
> Unfolded out of the sympathy of the woman is all sympathy;
> A man is a great thing upon the earth, and through
> eternity, but every jot of the greatness of man is unfolded
> out of woman;

> *First the man is shaped in the woman, he can then be*
> *shaped in himself.*

I once wrote a prayer that cast "Our Father" into "Our Mother." Whenever I recite it, I silently dedicate it to my mother who gave me love and my own life.

OUR MOTHER

Our Mother who is Nature,
We celebrate your loving-kindness.

Your earth is beautiful and bountiful.
Your love is without limit,
And fills all Creation and all time.

May we share the bounty you give us,
so no one wants.
And may our love be without limit
also.

May we create a community of fairness
and equality
Where compassion and love
bring harmony of self
and peace among neighbors
and nations.

Edward Searl

For what is yours
You give us so freely.

Your bounty and beauty
And neverending love.

Amen

*Don't be inhibited. You're a miracle. You're the
center of a unique world. Put a favorite photograph or
photographs of yourself progressing through the years on
this altar along with objects that represent you. Do you
have a complimentary note or letter someone sent you?
Include objects you love—their beauty reflects your
beauty. Add representations of your accomplishments.*

We all know how important self-esteem is.
We also know how easy it is to mistake
self-centeredness for self-esteem. I believe that a healthy sense of self is at the heart of
personal spirituality.

It's a natural progression to celebrate the self after honoring Mother love. Isn't the purpose of being
a mother to nurture a unique and valuable new human Life through unconditional love?

The following selections offer insight into your
spiritual being, so you may celebrate the self in confidence, joy, and gratitude. Dare to celebrate your
own self, but be vigilant against self-centeredness.

Begin your reflection on the spiritual nature of

the self with a selection by a poet of the human spirit, Walt Whitman.

Each of us inevitable,
Each of us limitless—each of us with his or
her right upon the earth,
Each of us allow'd the eternal purports of
the earth,
Each of us here as divinely as any is here.

Praise the intentions of your Creator—the Divine design that is your body, mind, and soul—through a prayer as valid today as when it was first spoken a century and a half ago by Theodore Parker.

We thank thee for our body, this handful of dust so curiously and wonderfully framed together.
We bless thee for this sparkle of thy fire that we call our soul, which enchants the dust into thoughtful human Life.
We thank thee for the varied powers thou hast given us here on earth:

the far-reaching mind, which puts all things underneath our feet, rides on the winds and the waters, and tames the lightning into useful service;
the use and the beauty which our thoughtful minds create, the grass of use for humble needs, the

bread of beauty for loftier and more aspiring powers;
 this conscience, whereby face to face we com-
mune with thine everlasting justice;
 the strength of will which can overpower the
weakness of mortal flesh, face danger and endure
hardship.

The progression of a well-lived Life begins with and returns to the center of the self. When we return to the center of self at the end of our Life's journey, we have found the universal that includes all humanity, Nature, and the Divine within our soul.

THREE JOURNEYS

The first journey
is inward:
Its adventure
is the discovery
of the self.
Self-knowledge,
is its end.
And it leads outward.

The second journey
is outward.
Its adventure
is the discovery of others.

Compassion and empathy,
a sense of involvement and understanding
are its ends.
And it leads inward.

The third journey
is inward again.
Its adventure
is the discovery of the Universal/Eternal,
a sense of wonder and mystery
are its ends.
And it leads Outward.

A Memorial Day altar calls for a bouquet of many flowers and a small American flag. Add photographs and mementos of your beloved whose memory you wish to honor. Make this altar joyous. You honor your beloved's devotions and sacrifices so you might have Life and enjoy Life.

Memorial Day was once known as Decoration Day, referring to the custom of sprucing up and placing flowers on graves—originally graves of Civil War veterans. In fact, two Union veterans began practicing the observance in 1866 in Waterloo, New York, and it quickly spread.

Nineteenth-century America, known for its "culture of death," took to this memorial observance—on the other side of the year from the church's deep autumn, All Saints Day. Customs of decorating graves, holding solemn parades, and listening to speeches have mostly disappeared. I've been fortunate to experience vestiges of Decoration Day traditions in small Midwestern towns.

Some towns still decorate cemeteries with heroic corridors of red, white, and blue flags and hold cemetery ceremonies. Veteran groups, military color guards, and high school bands march. Volleys are fired into the sky, to resound in the late morning quiet.

Whenever I witness such ceremonies, I feel mixed emotions. It's good to honor those who've died in service to their country's ideals. But I can't deny the deep tragedy of so many premature deaths, the horror and stupidity of war. I offer a prayer of thanksgiving for peace—a peace utterly tangible in a rural Midwestern cemetery surrounded by young corn plants receding to all horizons. I rededicate myself to working for peace.

HARD TO IMAGINE

In late spring
When the grass grows green
and trees are heavy-leafed,
When the buckeye blooms
and the air is fragrant with many flowers,
It is hard to imagine
there is such a thing as destruction.

In late spring,
When maple seeds spin to the ground
and fledglings venture from the nest,
When acorns sprout at tiny oaks

and birds sing at four in the morning,
It is hard to imagine
there is such a thing as death.

And this is even harder to imagine
In the green and flower and life
of late spring:
That there is such a thing as war,
That we, creatures capable of reason and love,
bring destruction and death
to one another.

This thing we call war—
this is the hardest to imagine
in late spring.

The old customs had a quiet truth in their annual attending to the resting places of the dead. It was inevitable that Decoration Day went beyond decorating only the graves of Civil War soldiers to include all graves.

Late May is a time for an optimistic tribute to those we loved, who prepared the way for us, and who are dead. To spruce up and decorate graves with flowers pays respect and affirms Life's continuity.

Some of us are able to visit graves of our ancestors and leave a token of flowers. But many of us live too far from those graves or perhaps there isn't a grave to visit.

Dedicate a part of your Memorial Day morning to offer your

own tribute. Set your altar with a bouquet of spring flowers and a small flag. Add mementos and photographs. Revisit in your memory places you shared with your beloved—old neighborhoods, a family church, a favorite restaurant, a museum, a park. Reminisce. Read a favorite passage you associate with your beloved. This is a good altar to share with family and friends.

The possibilities of your own Memorial Day remembrances are many—as varied and as rich as your association with the one or many you memorialize. Such a yearly observance, in the season of youthful Nature, gives you the permission to live throughout the rest of the year. The following selection by Wilbur Willey speaks of Memorial Day as "a signal to get on with important things."

In May, when the plots are well-cut and trimmed, when flowers are blooming naturally, when new flags blow brightly on the graves of veterans, when a parade goes by and a brass band plays, this is not a scene of sadness, of death, or even of remembering. It is a rebirth, a renewal, and a celebration, and a signal to get on with the important things of our own living.

Here there is above all pride and love, and places and things done in a social way are signs of connectedness—of ourselves to our past, of ourselves to our destiny. I can't think of anything more optimistic than the planting of a flower, than the response to a light wind and a song, than the consideration of one another for a shared experience.

Week 24
Such a Love!

This altar is a shrine to that person who has made love real for you and has fulfilled your desire. Begin with a favorite photograph of your beloved. Dedicate a beautiful bouquet to this person—splurge with a bouquet of roses. A home-grown bouquet has special significance. Light candles in your most beautiful candleholders.

June—a month of romance, love, and weddings—is a good time to celebrate your desire for another person and that person's desire for you. A giving and taking of physical love is one of Life's greatest joys and when that is combined with real love, well, you have *such a love!*

Honor such a love in your life. Delight in it, if you're in love's throes. Recall it, if you've drifted into familiarity in your intimate relationship. Restore it, if love has gone from your life.

Such a love, combining the physical and sacred, is spiritual.

Edward Searl

A WHITE ROSE

The red rose whispers of passion,
And the white rose breathes of love;
Oh, the red rose is a falcon,
And the white rose is a dove.

But I send you a cream-white rosebud
With a flush on its petal tips;
For the love that is purest and sweetest
Has a kiss of desire on the lips.
—*John Boyle O'Reilly*

I set my altar with a single white rose blushed with red, not only to reflect on the symbolism of this poem, but also in remembrance of a rose with this verse attached that I gave thirty years ago to the woman who became my wife.

Two additional selections, proven by time, reinforce the possibility of *sacred passion*. The first selection, verses by Robert Burns, uses a timeless symbolism.

A RED, RED ROSE

O my Luve's like a red, red rose,
That's newly spring in June;
O my Luve's like the melodie
That's sweetly play'd in tune—

> As fair art thou, my bonie lass,
> So deep in luve am I;
> And I will love thee still, my Dear,
> till a' the seas gang dry—
>
> Till a' the seas gan dry, my Dear,
> And the rock melt wi' the sun:
> I will love thee still, my Dear,
> While the sands o' Life shall run.
>
> And fare thee weel, my only Luve!
> And fare thee weel, a while!
> And I will come again, my Luve,
> Tho' it were ten thousand mile!

The second selection by the Puritan poet Anne Bradstreet ascends to heights of spiritual love sustained through a committed relationship.

TO MY DEAR AND LOVING HUSBAND

> If ever two were one, then surely we.
> If ever man were loved by wife, then thee.
> If ever wife was happy in a man,
> Compare with me, ye women, if you can.
> I prize thy love more than whole mines of gold,
> Or all the riches that the East doth hold.
> My love is such that rivers cannot quench,

Edward Searl

Nor ought but love from thee give recompense.
Thy love is such I can no way repay;
The heavens reward thee manifold, I pray.
Then while we live, in love let's so persevere
That when we live not more, we may live ever.

Verses from the Bible's Song of Solomon also further affirm the rightness of a love that touches the body as well as the soul.

Behold, thou art fair, my love,
behold, thou art fair;
I am my beloved's and my beloved
is mine . . .

Make haste my beloved . . .
(KJV, S. of Sol. 4:1, 6:3, 8:14)

This devotion honors the sort of living that shapes and smooths, in a positive sense, the wear and tear of experience. You may, as I have, accumulated a cache of tumbled stones gathered on a beach or along a river. Place those on your altar and consider what attracted you to them. You can also add some cherished object worn from much use. You might even have kept a worn, stuffed animal from your childhood.

I've spent hundreds of hours walking along Lake Superior's rock-littered, wave-battered, isolated shores. At the water's edge I hunt agates, semi-precious stones with beautiful bands of transparent color. The agates I find are smaller than eggs and often smooth and shiny from years, maybe centuries, of tumbling by surging storms and endless waves. Usually the smoothest agates with the most visible markings have little fractures from being smashed against other rocks. Though they're not gem quality, I love these agates just as I find them, because their beauty and their flaws result from Nature's great processes.

Their smoothness, the result of a long tumbling, is a lesson that I relate to my own life.

The venerable Skin Horse taught this lesson to the Velveteen Rabbit in Margery Williams's classic children's story, *The Velveteen Rabbit*. The Rabbit was trying to understand the notion of "real."

THE VELVETEEN RABBIT

"Real is not how you are made," said the Skin Horse. "It's a thing that happens to you. When a child really loves you for a long, long time, not just to play with, but REALLY loves you, then you become Real."

"Does it hurt?" asked the Rabbit.

"Sometimes," said the Skin Horse, for he was always truthful. "When you are Real you don't mind being hurt."

"Does it happen all at once, like being wound up," he asked, "or bit by bit?"

"It doesn't happen all at once," said the Skin Horse. "You become. It takes a long time. That's why it doesn't often happen to people who break easily, or have sharp edges, or who have to be carefully kept. Generally, by the time you are Real, most of your hair has been loved off, and your eyes drop out and you get loose in the joints and very shabby. But these things don't matter at all, because once you are Real you can't be ugly, except to people who don't understand."

The risks of living and loving are real risks. But the rewards can't be reaped without the risks and sometimes the failures and losses that result. Thomas John Carlisle explains why it is good to risk.

Our Jeopardy

It is good to use
best china
treasured dishes
the most genuine goblets
or the oldest lace tablecloth
there is a risk of course
every time we use anything
or anyone shares an inmost
mood or moment
or a fragile cup of revelation
but not to touch
not to handle
not to employ the available
artifacts of being
a human being
that is the quiet crash
the deadly catastrophe
where nothing
is enjoyed or broken
or spilled
or stained or mended
where nothing is ever
lived

loved
pored over
laughed over
wept over
lost
or found

One of the rewards of a Life lived fully is "a peace not past our understanding," described by John Holmes in this excerpt from "The People's Peace."

Days into years, the doorways worn at sill,
years into lives, the plans for long increase
come true at last for those of God's good will:
these are the things we mean by saying, Peace.

An Empty Basket

Keep this altar simple. Place on it a small empty basket. I don't even add a candle, because the flame would distract me from this devotion's counsel that before I seek fullness, I must first be empty.

This is one of my standard devotions because I'm often too full of myself or distracted. I need to be admonished again and again to be receptive.

In this book's grouping of devotions, I place this devotion at the end of spring, just before summer begins. I want to enter summer with a receptive heart, mind, and soul, to gather an abundance of summer sensations, experiences, and meanings.

An empty basket has been part of my own spiritual imagery for twenty years. Here's how that happened.

I was a new minister. That she hadn't liked my service clearly registered on her whole body—as rigid as the thin line of her lips. She reluctantly extended her hand to shake mine, but her words weren't hesitant. Her dark eyes grew intense. She complained, "I came seeking bread, and you gave me stones."

Crushed, confused, and yes, angry, I had no response.

Later I searched the Bible for the source of her admonishment. I found words of the tempter—the devil—who confronted Jesus in the wilderness after forty days and nights of fasting: "And when the tempter came to him, he said, 'If thou be the Son of God, command that these stones be made bread.' " (KJV, Matt. 4:3)

I thought: Wouldn't that have been a great comeback? I could have identified her with the devil by quoting from the very book she professed to love and in which she proclaimed me deficient.

But she wasn't the devil. She was a suffering soul. She was sick in spirit. She suffered from bouts of depression. Her loyalties lay with the minister whom I'd replaced. Her marriage was disintegrating.

I sought to understand her. I eventually found a key in a venerable colleague's droll collection of parables.

> *Behold there cometh to the Master of the Temple a certain man that complaineth bitterly, saying, "On every Sabbath day do I come to the Temple: Sometimes is my spirit renewed within me, but more often do I come empty away. I ask for bread, and thou offerest me only a stone."*
>
> *And the master of the Temple asked him, saying, "Thou dost come to the Temple expecting to be fed*

> *with bread each and every time thou comest?" And*
> *the man answered, "Nay, not every time that I come*
> *to the Temple." Then spake the Master of the Tem-*
> *ple, saying, "Thou has the answer to thine own com-*
> *plaint, for only they that come each time with*
> *expectation, bringing with them their empty baskets,*
> *beareth away the bread of Life." [Clinton Lee Scott,*
> *Parish Parables]*

This story gives me insight into this woman in particular, but more, it taught me about a type of person—one who is un-receptive, untouchable. It gave me insight into myself. I re-alized that sometimes I am unreceptive, untouchable. When this is so, I unconsciously thwart receiving the Bread of Life I desire.

Too often, in too many situations, I do not bring an empty basket: I have no basket. Or my basket is already full and will hold no more. Or I expect someone else to turn the stones already in my basket into bread.

In a recent Sunday service I used a contemporary reading referring to a "Buddhist monk's begging bowl." The story had such an effect on listeners that I received two very handsome and meaningful handmade gifts: a small ceramic bowl and the small woven basket.

I appreciate both gifts. For me, each holds a particular nuance of meaning. An empty basket and a beggar's bowl have similarities but also an essential difference. The empty

151

basket does not implicitly renounce desire as the beggar's bowl does.

I often place the little basket on my altar when I have no specific devotion. The little basket signifies my intense desire for spiritual nourishment—the Bread of Life. It reminds me of a mindset I must bring to worship and integrate into my actions, if I am to get the nourishment of spirit I crave. If I am to receive the Bread of Life I must become an empty basket.

The little empty basket focuses me in the morning and throughout the day. It's an allegory of my spiritual potential and an aspiration that I become what is represented.

READY TO RECEIVE

Carefully wrought,
Cunningly woven,
Light and strong,
Symmetrical,
And balanced:
I am an empty basket
Ready to receive
The Bread of Life
In every moment,
From every person
And grace of Creation.

summer

This altar remembers and expands on the previous week's devotion of an empty basket. Place a large basket on your altar. A curving cornucopia shape welcomes the abundance of the season. Fill the basket to overflowing with fresh vegetables, maybe with the tops still on and earth clinging to them. Strew flowers, leaves, and grasses around the candles you light.

Summer has a timeless quality—a welcome illusion. Dawn arrives early and night falls late. All of Nature grows deeply and silently. Summer seems immortal. Embrace this season, as summer has embraced life on earth for millions of years.

IT'S SUMMER NOW

The days are long now.
It is hot. Before
The rain, thunder rumbles
From darkly sculptured
Clouds. In the night, mist
Drifts in the lowlands.

The moon casts beguiling,
Cool shadows. This is
How it has been for
Millennia,
Longer than our race
Can remember.

Vegetation grows
Lushly. The air is
Fragrant with many
Aromas. Insects fly.
Young fish dart in the
Shallows. Fledglings try
Their unpracticed wings.
The warm-blooded young
Test the resiliency
Of the padded earth.
This, too, is how it
Has been for millennia,
Longer than our race
Can remember.

The days are long now.
Life swells.
It is a
Wonder and a joy.

Summer moves slowly. Adjust your rhythms to Nature's rhythms. Give yourself many occasions to enjoy summer moments and experiences. When you labor, work with focus, intention, and pleasure. Allow yourself ample time for recreation—to restore yourself and to do what you have passion for. Envision Nature as a cornucopia.

CORNUCOPIA

Summer is a cornucopia,
A great curving horn of plenty,
Spilling Life's bounty—
Unhurried days and velvety nights,
Towering clouds
uniting earth and heaven,
Sunshine so buttery
it greases your fingers,
Slow afternoons suspended in time,
Thick leaves and fragrant grasses,
Puddles of cool shade,
Armfuls of flowers,
Vegetables ripening and fruits swelling.

As they spill,
Gather these tumbling blessings
In the receptive basket of self.

The cornucopia cannot be emptied.
You cannot be filled.

Add to your altar your small empty basket from the previous week's altar. What I wish for you, I can't give. It's yours to take. Accept all of it gladly.

SUMMER WISHES, FOR YOU

I wish for you an abundant summer:
a season of many sensations and experiences;
a season of re-creation;
a season that transmutes
the promise of spring
into the harvest of autumn.
I wish for you good health, enthusiasm,
and a growing wisdom.

I wish you a long summer, a languorous summer—
a long journey home. . . .

Set this altar as you would a table for a special guest. You are that special guest. Use a beautiful cloth, a delicate china cup, a graceful teapot, shining candlesticks, graceful tapers, and an elegant but simple arrangement of flowers. Add a stick of fragrant incense. If tea isn't your preferred beverage, still use your best and most beautiful glasses.

Late afternoon, when the sun approaches the western horizon and long shafts of light sluice over the earth to illuminate what had been shadowed, is a time to pause. Allow yourself to gather poignant feelings, indulge simple pleasures, and meditate with the help of things that create a distinct mood, unlike the mood of any other time of day. Late afternoon and early evening are liminal—a threshold of religious experience. It's a time to savor the complex bouquet of Life.

Thirteen centuries ago a renowned Chinese poet, Tu Fu, captured the timelessness of a late afternoon mood in a poem.

SUNSET

Sunset glitters on the beads
Of the curtains. Spring flowers
Bloom in the valley. The gardens
Along the river are filled
With perfume. Smoke of cooking
Fires drifts over the slow barges.
Sparrows hop and tumble in
The branches. Whirling insects
Swarm in the air. Who discovered
That one cup of thick wine
Will dispel a thousand cares?
    [translator *Kenneth Rexroth*]

A cup of tea, a mug of coffee, even a glass of ginger ale, when made into a little ceremony, can dispel a thousand cares, embracing the late afternoon experience. I like to set an afternoon altar with a pot of hot tea and a stick of fragrant incense, arranged so the steam from the spout mixes with the smoke rising from the incense. My thoughts rise in a beguiling dance. I sip my tea, aware of its warmth and flavor. The aroma of the incense lingers, stretching out the afternoon illusion of suspended time. I'm reminded of William James's description of afternoon tea as a "little eternity."

A Place of Your Own

FROM PORTRAIT OF A LADY

*Under certain circumstances there are few hours in life more
agreeable than the hour dedicated to the ceremony known as
afternoon tea. There are circumstances in which, whether you
partake of the tea or not—some people of course never do—
the situation is in itself delightful. Those that I have in mind
in the beginning to unfold this simple history offered an ad-
mirable setting to an innocent pastime. The implements of
the little feast had been disposed upon the lawn of an old
English country-house, in what I should call the perfect middle of a splendid summer afternoon. Part of the afternoon had
waned, but much of it was left, and what was left was of the
finest and rarest quality. Real dusk would not arrive for many
hours; but the flood of summer light had begun to ebb, the
air had grown mellow, the shadows were long upon the
smooth, dense turf. They lengthened slowly, however, and the
scene expressed that sense of leisure still to come which is
perhaps the chief source of one's enjoyment of such a scene
at such an hour. From five o'clock to eight is on certain occasions a little eternity; but on such an occasion as this the
interval could be only an eternity of pleasure.*

While the hour lends itself to the pleasurable phenomenon of
afternoon tea, the phenomenon is not exclusive to afternoon,
because it involves a state of mind.

Edward Searl

A STATE OF MIND

Afternoon tea is a state of mind.

Afternoon tea is the freedom to pause when the day has arrived at its very best. Nothing else seems to matter, because you are mindful in the moment.

Afternoon tea is ceremonial. Give it intention and attention: Boil the water, warm the pot, steep the tea leaves. Pour the brew into a fine cup. Inhale the fragrant steam rising from a mug of hot coffee. Hold the glass of wine to sunlight and appreciate the color, before taking the first sip. Mix the cocktail just so.

Contemplate the slanting rays of the afternoon sun and the motes dancing in them. Muse on flames dancing in a fireplace. Don't rush toward words.

Don't hurry. Don't fret. Your cares will drift away.

The moment is suspended in amber.

Afternoon tea, white space in time, gives definition to other times of the day.

Any life too busy or hectic so as not to include afternoon tea needs adjustment.

Consider yourself as wealthy as you have occasions of afternoon tea.

Prepare for this altar by selecting a crusty, yeasty bread and a wine you find particularly flavorful—I use a red. Place the bread on a simple plate and pour the wine into a simple glass. Votive candles will cast a flickering, sanctifying light on the bread and wine and not distract as a taller candle might.

The best blessings give us what we already have. You see, I believe that we're already and always blessed: Blessed to have Life. Blessed to be a human being with a marvelous mind to think and dexterous hands to create. Blessed by fellow human beings to love and be loved by. Blessed by Nature with abundant beauty, sensations, and counsel.

The best blessings insinuate an active and heartfelt gratitude. The Gift Giver wants us to enjoy and delight in the blessings so liberally given. To do otherwise is both a lack of wisdom and lack of faith.

I have a favorite blessing that comes from an ancient and curious book—Ecclesiastes of the Old Testament. Ecclesiastes belongs to the wisdom tradition.

It is a collection of sayings loosely joined together. Ecclesiastes asks questions but doesn't speculate. Its wisdom is conventional—distilled from the timeless human condition. It draws a singular conclusion that in spite of all things considered and evidence to the contrary, Life is good and it was intended to be lived. Ecclesiastes offers this blessing.

> *Go, eat your bread with enjoyment, and drink your wine with a merry heart; for God has already approved what you do.*
>
> *Let your garments be always white; let not oil be lacking on your head.*
>
> *Enjoy life with the wife whom you love, all the days of your vain life which he has given you under the sun, because that is your portion in life and in your toil at which you toil under the sun. Whatever your hand finds to do, do it with your might. (RSV, Eccles. 9:7–9)*

The bread and wine on this altar symbolize the blessings of Creation.

The bread represents human sustenance—Nature joined to industry; and it represents the basics of which we are well provided. The wine represents these things, too, and something more—an ecstatic extra. Creation hasn't designed us to plod along, but to step lightly, to welcome companions, to meet challenges, and to revel in much beauty. In mindfulness and gratitude, "Eat your bread with enjoyment, and drink your wine with a merry heart, for God has already approved what you do."

This devotion suggests many possible settings, find one that resonates with you. In preparation, think of things that inspire your awe: a chambered nautilus shell, cut in half to reveal its cunning spiral, a fossil millions of years old, a prism that refracts light into a rainbow of color, a photograph of the Milky Way, the face of a child. . . . Place one such thing or several such things on your altar.

An essential spiritual orientation is a well-developed sense of wonder. A person who has a sense of wonder is rarely bored, never alienated, and invariably optimistic, because to her the world is wonderful!

You can return a sense of wonder to your spiritual life by really seeing what your eyes already behold. Create a sense of urgency: Whatever you see, imagine you're seeing it either for the first or last time. This strategy will expose the extraordinary that is ever present in the ordinary.

Rachel Carson wrote about a summer's night

when she realized that most of us, most of the time, fail to really see with wondering eyes.

FROM THE SENSE OF WONDER

. . . It was a clear night without a moon. With a friend, I went out on a flat headland that is almost a tiny island, being all but surrounded by the waters of the bay. . . . We lay and looked up at the sky and the millions of stars that blazed in darkness. The night was so still that we could hear the buoy on the ledges out beyond the mouth of the bay. Once or twice a word spoken by someone on the far shore was carried across on the clear air. A few lights burned in cottages. Otherwise there was no reminder of other human life; my companion and I were alone with the stars. I have never seen them more beautiful: the misty river of the Milky Way flowing across the sky, the patterns of constellations standing out bright and clear, a blazing planet low on the horizon. Once or twice a meteor burned its way into the earth's atmosphere.

It occurred to me that if this were a sight that could be seen only once in a century or seen once in a generation, this little headland would be thronged with spectators. But it can be seen many scores of nights in any year, and so the lights burned in the cottages and the inhabitants probably gave not a thought to the beauty overhead; and because they could see it almost any night perhaps they will never see it.

Ralph Waldo Emerson made the same observation and reached a similar conclusion.

If the stars should appear one night in a thousand, how we would believe and adore, and preserve for many generations the remembrance of the City of God which had been shown. But every night come out these envoys of beauty, and light the universe with their admonishing smile.

Summer has so many lush sensations, the days are so long, and they move so slowly it's easy to take it all for granted. If you have a sense of wonder in this most wonderful season, great rewards wait for you.

I WISH YOU WONDER

I wish you wonder:
Wonder that vanquishes
cynicism,
Wonder that sees deeper
than the surface of things.
Wonder that releases the heart
and expands the mind,
Wonder that gives awareness
of self and of others
Joined together—strangely—
in this Great Adventure of Life.

Edward Searl

May your eyes see;
May your ears hear;
May all your senses be
alert and keen,
Leading you into and beyond wonder
To the most holy of holies,
the very center,
the essence of Life.

A Long Falling in Love

You have one relationship at the center of your life—a relationship that you and the other person have vowed to keep through the bad times as well as the good times. Set your altar to celebrate this committed relationship even as you look at it realistically. Begin with a photograph of you and your beloved. Add candlelight and flowers. You might place your wedding ring here, too, to remember the promises you made, the circle of your love and all that you've been through together.

Through most of the year a relentless current carries us along a channel of routine and work. Summer's moods and vacations offer a vantage that puts the rest of the year in perspective. On a summer holiday time spent alone with your spouse, perhaps in a new setting, can make you realize that you need to pay more attention to your primary relationship. Hold in your consciousness how much you've experienced and how much you've grown because of one another.

This devotion intimates that such a relationship

is a work in progress—a work that requires courage, endurance, and faith in your partner as well as in yourself. I've always appreciated what Anne Morrow Lindbergh wrote about fluid relationships in *Gifts from the Sea.*

FROM GIFT FROM THE SEA

When you love someone you do not love them all the time, in exactly the same way, from moment to moment. It is an impossibility. It is even a lie to pretend to. And yet, this is exactly what most of us demand. We have so little faith in the ebb and flow of life, of love, of relationships. We leap at the flow of the tide and resist in terror its ebb. We are afraid it will never return. We insist on permanency, on duration, on continuity; when the only continuity possible, in life as in love, is in growth, in fluidity—in freedom, in the sense that the dancers are free, barely touching as they pass, but partners in the same pattern. The only real security is not in owning or possessing, not in demanding or expecting, not in hoping, even. Security in a relationship lies neither in looking back to what it was in nostalgia, nor forward to what it might be in dread or anticipation, but living in the present relationship and accepting it as it is now. For relationships, too, must be like islands. One must accept them for what they are here and now, within their limits— islands, surrounded and interrupted by the sea, and continually visited and abandoned by the tides. One must accept

the security of the winged life, of ebb and flow, of intermit-
tency.

The mark of a fluid relationship that is nevertheless committed
and enduring is a continual freshness. Theodore Parker, writing
in the nineteenth century, described marriage as a long falling
in love. We're married to our spouse day by day, a little more
by a little more. Place your wedding ring, a symbol of patience
and endurance, on your altar and reflect on its symbolism.

It takes years to marry completely two hearts, even of the most
loving and well-assorted. A happy wedlock is a long falling in
love. Young persons think love belongs only to the brown-
haired and crimson-cheeked. So it does for its beginning. But
the golden marriage is part of love which the bridal day knows
nothing of.

A perfect and complete marriage, where wedlock is every-
thing you could ask and the ideal of marriage becomes actual,
is not common, perhaps as rare as perfect personal beauty.
Men and women are married fractionally, now a small frac-
tion, then a large fraction. Very few are married totally, and
then only after some forty or fifty years of gradual approach
and experiment.

Such a large and sweet fruit is a complete marriage that
it needs a long summer to ripen in, and then a long winter
to mellow and season it. But a real, happy marriage of love
and judgment between a noble man and woman is one of the
things so very handsome that if the sun were, as the Greek

poets fabled, a god, he might stop the world and hold it still now and then in order to look all day long on some example thereof, and feast his eyes on such a spectacle.

Look at your marriage as a journey, an odyssey of adventure and fulfillment, yet fraught with difficulties and perils. This journey involves the discovery and deep knowledge of another person as complex as you are complex, and of being discovered and known in the same way.

A GREAT ADVENTURE

There are many adventures—
journeys that take us
through our days.
One of the most
mysterious and rewarding,
yet accessible and undervalued adventures
Is the journey two persons take together
On roads that converge, run parallel,
and loop seemingly away
only to refind their course
to converge again and again.

This is the journey of self-discovery,
deep knowledge of another, shared purposes,
a building together, and fluid love.

A Place of Your Own

*This is the adventure so common
we sometimes neglect and often forget
the courage and the wisdom it takes—
and gives.*

This devotion considers two aspects of spiritual re-
flection I experience over and over again: the divinity
that creates, sustains, and contains Creation and our
human identity with that divinity. I place a most an-
cient representation of divinity—a photograph of a
huge orange sun perched on an ocean horizon—on
this altar. You might have a favorite Nature photo-
graph that stirs in you what is often called a "cosmic
consciousness."

I drive through miles and miles of Midwestern
farmland in full summer—the sunlight strong,
fields lush with corn and soybeans, the earth
dark and solid—and repeat a magnificent yet simple
revelation. The revelation seems as fresh as when it
first came to me: Creation is a Unity. Nature ema-
nates from one Source, and all aspects of Nature
converge in one Source. That Source dwells in all
aspects of Nature. Nature reposes in the Source.
Sometimes in July or August, when at sunset the sun
is a great orange sphere and seems to rest on the
horizon, this idea becomes palpable.

I've had this revelation throughout my life in many places and many situations, and it isn't unique to me. My favorite expression of it comes from the writing of Ralph Waldo Emerson arranged by Arthur Foote II.

THE OVERSOUL

Let us learn the revelation of all nature and thought; that the Highest dwells within us, that the sources of nature are in our own minds.

As there is no screen or ceiling between our heads and the infinite heavens, so there is no bar or wall in the soul where we, the effect, cease, and God, the cause, begins.

I am constrained every moment to acknowledge a higher origin for events than the will I call mine.

There is deep power in which we exist and whose beatitude is accessible to us.

Every moment when the individual feels invaded by it is memorable.

It comes to the lowly and simple; it comes to whomsoever will put off what is foreign and proud; it comes as insight; it comes as serenity and grandeur.

The soul's health consists in the fullness of its reception.

For ever and ever the influx of this better and more universal self is new and unsearchable.

Within us is the soul of the whole, the wise silence, the universal beauty, to which every part and particle is equally related; the Eternal One.

When it breaks through our intellect, it is genius; when it breathes through our will, it is virtue; when it flows through our affection, it is love.

The identity of the individual with the Divine Source—an identity shared with all that is beautiful, true, and good—is beautifully and timelessly expressed in Hinduism's *Bhagavad Gita.*

BRAHMAN

I am: never born and without beginning.
Neither gods nor sages know my Source.
I am their Source.

Every being emerges from my Being.
Every soul is a small part of my limitless Soul.

I am the Father and Mother of the universe.

I am the beginning, the Span of Years,
and the end of all beings.

I am Birth, Death, the Sustainer, and the Way.

I am Time without beginning or end.

Wherever you look I am.

A Place of Your Own

All attributes of existence are my Attributes:
intelligence and memory, knowledge and wisdom,
pleasure and pain, self-control and serenity,
fame and infamy, fear and courage.

I am the Divine Seed. Nothing exists
except through me. All evolves
out of me.

All glory, all beauty, all prosperity,
and all power comes from me,
yet is only a fragment of my Glory.

I pervade the whole Universe
with this fragment of my Self.

Set this altar with a single candle in an artful holder. Place several seashells around the candle as symbols of the gifts that come with patience and faith. By staring into the flame your vision will find a deep, objectless focus that soothes the mind and opens the unconscious.

I n *Gifts from the Sea*, Anne Morrow Lindbergh described a process by which a vacationer falls under the spell of seashore rhythms. The conscious mind gradually relinquishes its customary concerns and becomes "empty, open, choiceless." After a week or so the mind wakens to a new awareness and insights begin to tumble from the unconscious into the conscious mind, like shells tossed on the smooth sand of a beach. She counsels that in order for this to happen one must have "patience and faith."

The discipline of silence follows a similar process: a gradual relinquishing of your customary consciousness, an awakening to a new awareness, and, if you're fortunate, significant insights rising from your unconscious mind. A summer holiday is well-suited to explore the discipline of silence. You have the right conditions and plenty of time. You need only to apply yourself faithfully and diligently.

Carl Scovel expands on the attitude that Anne Morrow Lindberg described.

Silence creates possibility—the possibility of hearing. What we learn to do—in silence—is to create within ourselves silence, to create within ourselves darkness, to create within ourselves emptiness, to become nobodies—to brush aside all words, all concepts, all feelings, all fantasies, all anxieties, all ambition—gently to brush away all these things that seem so important—to let them go and to empty ourselves so that if the word is spoken we may hear it, and if the song is sung we may attend.

In silence we do not try to be anything or anyone—we do not try to be wise, or pious, or brave, or witty, or mature— we give up trying to be and simply are—we become being— or put it another way we become nothing in order that we may once again become that which we truly are. In silence we rest as the child rests in its mother's arms and we are fed as the child nurses at its mother's breast. I assure you that no matter who you are or what you do—the practice of silence may be the single most real and helpful thing you do each day.

You may find sitting in silence difficult. You're not alone, as Arthur Foote noted.

Most of us dread going "into the silence." We have lost the ability profitably to be alone—lost it through disuse, like the burrowing mole who has become blind. If we retire to be alone, it is no delight. Our minds do a hop, skip, and jump; we find ourselves unable to concentrate. The beds unmade, the letters unwritten set up a clamoring demand, and we experience none of the tranquility we have come apart to enjoy.

But this is only to say that the discipline of solitude is difficult, and our own disorganized condition, pitiful. The only remedy is to learn this art anew. We can only learn to swim by swimming; one can only learn the advantage of solitude by faithful practice. And, like swimmers, we must learn to not thrash about, but entrust ourselves to the buoyancy of the silence. For silence has a real buoyancy; and the power to collect our thoughts by withdrawal from the outward to the inward is the way to discover that life indeed "is a pure flame," and there is "an invisible sun within us" by which we truly live.

Overcome your reluctances. Dare to repose in silence. Embark on a meditative path.

MEDITATIVE JOURNEY

Be quiet,
as tumbling thoughts abate.

Be calm
as your racing pulse slackens.

In the quiet, in the calm,
Journey from the personal into the common,
from the particular into the collective.

Know your kinship
to humanity,
to Nature,
to the Cosmos.

Enter the realm
of the Universal and Timeless
Where meaning and peace are inseparable.

Hold that vision
as long as you are able,
So a residue of meaning and peace
will be with you
As your thoughts and feelings swell,
As your pulse quickens,
As you reenter this place and this time,
return to your Self, and go about your day.

Don't expect that the insights and deep peace of the discipline of silence will occur immediately or even soon, though the salutary benefits will be evident from the first. Practice this devotion regularly—even daily. Your altar will then become a place that induces a great peace—a sanctuary of your psyche.

Celebrating Your Children

Sort through photographs of your children. Select a few that evoke in you their individual essences and the evanescence of their years. Have you saved drawings, cards, and other things your children made? Add those to the photographs. For my daughter I add a bouquet of daisies that remind me of the day she was born.

Summer belongs to children. In summer a child can grow like a weed, physically becoming a new person in a matter of months.

Celebrate your children. See them as the unique individuals they are. Recognize what they've brought to your life. Set your altar with their photographs and mementos of your children. Remember special moments from your life together.

I have one daughter, Katy, who is now an adult. She and I had a mutual adoration society throughout her childhood and youth. When I look back on our years together, I realize how much she brought into my life. Her mere being expanded my capacity to love. Always to my amazement, she taught me through her openness and innocence, and by her attitudes and responses, even—perhaps especially—when she strained to be independent.

When I celebrate my daughter's August birthday, setting my altar with her photograph and objects she made both as a child and as a mature artist, I vividly recall times when she acted as my teacher. Let three of my stories serve to stimulate stories of your children.

When Katy was three years old she inspired "found" poems.

INNOCENCE REDISCOVERED

We gain foolishness
as we grow in age;
Yesterday's innocence
lost in tomorrow's sage.

With child moist eyes,
fresh from morning dew,
She looked in my eyes,
"Daddy, I like you!"

"Like? Why like, dear?"
Praise, adulation,
I wanted to hear
with cute intonation.
Instead,
she whispered in my ear
an essay in human relations:

> *"Beard.*
> *Chin.*
> *Mouth.*
> *Two dots.*
> *Glasses,*
> *Eyes. Eyelashes.*
> *Eyebrows.*
> *Hair.*
> *You smell nice.*
> *That's all I like about you,*
> *Daddy."*

A second story occurred when my daughter was a high school freshman.

It was a gray, rainy weekday evening in later winter. I was going to leave a pair of shoes to be heeled. "Will you get a can of coffee while you're out?" my wife asked. "If you don't there won't be any coffee in the morning." I felt put out by the request. And then my daughter decided to tag along because she had to get some school supplies she absolutely needed. I felt even more put out. A simple errand had turned into a shopping expedition!

At the supermarket I quickly purchased the coffee. I leaned against the shopping carts queued by the entrance—self-consciously patient while my daughter browsed the aisles and eventually made her purchase at a distant counter.

I watched customers enter the store, many obviously on

their way home from work. I mused about their lives. You know how easily thoughts swell and tumble on a rainy evening.

A father and high-school aged daughter entered, heads bent in conversation. Another daughter, a few years younger, trailed. She looked around with wide-eyed and wondering innocence that signified Down's Syndrome. As they passed, my eyes followed. I speculated—projecting from my own irritation—about the family's inconveniences, distresses, embarrassments.

And then, in a quicksilver movement, the older daughter slowed her pace just a little, the younger sister drew alongside. As though they were one person joining two hands, not two separate young women, their hands met and held. I swear they never exchanged the slightest glance. They were of one mind.

It was a gracious, tender sight. It had in it concern, trust, love, sisterhood . . . more than I can adequately describe. It was a moment of meaning whose meaning seeped into me.

As my daughter approached, my hand found hers.

Now an adult, Katy has an array of sensitivities and strengths. Whenever I envision her full and unique personality, I'm astounded. A year ago, when Katy was a young woman in her late twenties, we went to a wedding together.

The setting was the San Jose wedding of Katy's cousin, Kris, my wife Ellie's niece. At the reception, Ellie, Katy, and I sat with Ellie's mom. The food was slow coming, but the wine was plentiful. Everyone was jovial. Laughter and conversation blended with the music of Sinatra and Bennett singing soft, up-tempo ballads.

Eventually the best man offered a toast to the newly married couple. Then the bride's father, Ellie's older brother, honored the four grandmothers present and concluded by raising his glass to the grandfathers, now gone from the world.

At that moment my daughter, Katy, sitting across from me, began to sob—not so much uncontrollably as inconsolably. She blurted out something about feeling the presence of her grandfather Fred—Katy and Kris's grandfather who'd died several years before.

Through our twenty-eight years together, Katy has often amazed me with her innate sensitivities and instincts. This was one of the most remarkable expressions. She couldn't adequately express it later, except by saying how incredible the experience was. Remembering it, she cried again. "It was spiritual—the most spiritual moment I've ever had."

I think I can explain it. Katy and Kris as children had spent summers together at their grandparents' home in the Adirondack/Lake Champlain country. Their grandfather, Fred, was often a difficult man, but for Katy he was simply her grandfather. His presence had been looming—twined with the magic and mystery of her childhood. When he died perhaps she didn't mourn his death as she needed to. Perhaps none of us did. She loved him unconditionally. His spirit was, figuratively at least, restless; and she was the most likely member of his family to be visited by him at this rare and perhaps last occasion when all the family was together. I posit all this in a psychological, not in a literal sense. But psyche is synonymous with soul and all of this has vague borders within the human mind's incredible possibilities and realities: personal, transpersonal, and universal; memory, imagination, intuition, and insight.

I didn't doubt at that moment nor do I doubt it now, that Katy, through the power of her memory and love, brought Fred into that moment—probably in a way that he would have always wanted but had never realized in the course of his life. Fred knew which of his progeny to visit not only to get entry but also to tap the unconditional love he craved.

*Choose a photograph or print of a diverse crowd—
a mix of ages, sexes, cultures, and races—to place upon
this altar. A beach scene would be particularly fitting
in this devotion, such as the one you imagine from
reading "Beautiful People."*

I love cities for a most obvious reason: the mass
and variety of people. I stare at faces and try to
comprehend what it is I share with this diversity
of human beings. We are all different in specifics, yet
we share general characteristics and a common destiny. Our individual spirits converge in an overarching Human Spirit.

*A memorable experience occurred for me one sum-
mer afternoon in downtown Vancouver. A street
musician—middle-aged, very Irish, and wearing a
heavy tweed suit—played a guitar and sang. He
grimaced and contorted with every note played,
pained by the intensity of his passion.*

I leaned against a bench and listened to him

sing four songs. The performance absorbed me. I lost track of time.

The songs ended. As though awakening from a rapture, my vision was sharp. I became acutely aware of the passerbys: business men and women in expensive, tailored suits carrying shiny leather folios; Chinese and West Indians; very British looking women with porcelain complexions, wearing gloves and hats that matched their dresses; street people, shopping bags bulging with their worldly possessions; adolescents with dyed and buzzed hair.

Then the music that had drifted into the back of my conscious came to the foreground. The Irish guitarist was singing "Let It Be," and the song's refrain bored into my consciousness.

At that moment I knew without a doubt the wisdom of acceptance and yielding—that being hard, stiff, and resisting is always the way of death and never the way of life. The song ended. I didn't need to hear more. I wanted to flow with and be pulled by the tide of humanity. I began to walk, drifting along sidewalks and crossing streets—one with the pulse of that wonderful mix of people I'd been watching.

It wasn't just that moment. It wasn't just the people of Vancouver I'd joined. I was part of all humanity, flowing through all time. I felt identity and empathy as never before.

Proclaim the wonderfulness of being human. If you realize your own worth and dignity, by empathy you will know the worth and dignity of every person. Clinton Lee Scott had a Universalist's vision of human beings.

BEAUTIFUL PEOPLE

All persons are beautiful.

Some are beautiful of form or face,
of carriage, or voice, and
all are beautiful with the beauty of human kind.

Persons of all ages are beautiful;
the child, the youth, those of middle age,
and those of many years.

The near naked girl upon the beach,
and the "little old lady in tennis shoes"
are both beautiful.

Beautiful the old man in his wheel chair,
the mother leading her child,
and the woman carrying her unborn
beneath her heart.

Beautiful the bride on her lover's arm,
and the laborer in overalls
going to his job.

*O, all you beautiful people, can you not see
the beauty in one another?*

We tend to emphasize relatively trivial superficial distinctions, and neglect the deeper, universal truths of a shared humanity. I believe there is spiritual meaning—a "Communion of Our Humanness"—in the human condition.

COMMUNION OF OUR HUMANNESS

*We make too much
of our distinctions,
That which separates and divides
one from another—
person from person,
race from race,
nation from nation—
you from me.*

*Beyond all that
separates and divides,
Beyond the superficial distinctions
of sex, age, color, origin,
religion, ability, whatever!
There is the communion
of our humanness.
Our instincts and impulses,
Our desires and drives,*

A Place of Your Own

Our hopes and fears
Are essentially the same.

We are kindred beings, soul mates,
brothers and sisters—
Of the same flesh and spirit.

I am my brother's and my sister's keeper,
I will do unto others as I would have done
to myself,
Because I am my brother and my sister
multiplied by the factor of all
my brothers and sisters who have lived,
who will ever live, and who live now.

Gather in a great basket a bouquet of seasonal vegetables—beautiful specimens of this vegetable and that vegetable. Vivid reminders of the bounty of Nature and the gifts of human industry, this harvest will also help you realize a bounty and diversity of friends, as you read the following devotion.

Humanity, an abstraction, may be hard for you to grasp and, in a spiritual sense, to celebrate. But the circle of people you know is real. Among them are friends. Friendship is a spiritual relationship that dispels loneliness and leads to self-knowledge.

There are degrees of friendship. When we think of friendship, we often focus on our closest friends. These are usually just a few—a best friend, a bosom buddy, or a kindred spirit.

The following litany by Max Coots—a thanksgiving of friends—sharpens our vision about friends and friendship and invariably reminds us of the treasure we have in those relationships. They are akin to the bounty of late summer.

A Place of Your Own

LET US GIVE THANKS

Let us give thanks for a bounty of people:

*For generous friends with hearts as big as hubbards and
smiles as bright as their blossoms;*

For feisty friends as tart as apples;

*For continuous friends, who, like scallions and cucumbers,
keep reminding us that we've had them;*

*For crotchety friends, as sour as rhubarb and as
indestructible;*

*For handsome friends, who are as gorgeous as eggplants and
as elegant as a row of corn, and the others, as plain as
potatoes and as good for you;*

*For funny friends, who are as silly as Brussels sprouts and as
amusing as Jerusalem artichokes, and serious friends, as
complex as cauliflowers and as intricate as onions;*

*For friends as unpretentious as cabbage, as subtle as
summer squash, as persistent as parsley, as delightful as
dill, as endless as zucchini, and who, like parsnips, can
be counted on to see you throughout the winter;*

195

*For old friends, nodding like sunflowers in the evening-
time, and young friends coming on as fast as radishes;*

*For loving friends, who wind around us like tendrils and
hold us, despite our blights, wilts, and witherings;*

*And finally for friends now gone, like gardens past that have
been harvested, and who fed us in their times that we
might have life thereafter;*

For all these we give thanks.

These Things I Have Loved

Just look around. Things you've chosen fill your home. Some of those things you love for their beauty and also for the associations they bring to you. In the broadest sense they are souvenirs—memorable keepsakes—from your life. Select a few of those things to put upon your altar. Fill a vase with flowers. Light candles in favorite candlesticks.

Summer is the season when I've acquired many of the things I possess—souvenirs of my holidays and wanderings. I once lusted after many things, now stashed away in closets, basement, and garage. The onset of midlife signaled the end of my avid acquisitiveness. Now I'm trying to simplify and streamline my existence, and I divest myself of things. In the process of sorting and discarding, I've pondered what these things have meant to me. I agree with Antoine St. d'Exupery who once wrote that "We live not by things, but by the meaning of things."

I set this altar with things I've loved and collected—agates gathered from Lake Superior's shore,

Edward Searl

photographs of places I've visited, a Blue Ridge plate from my motley collection of several hundred pieces I found in second-hand stores, a well-thumbed paperback anthology of Emerson's epigrams.

In a curious way, I have a love of the things that have filled my life, though my desire to possess them has diminished. A favorite poem, Rupert Brooke's "The Great Lover," leaps to mind when I think about *things*.

FROM THE GREAT LOVER

These I have loved:
White plates and cups, clean-gleaming
ringed with blue lines; and feathery, faery dust;
Wet roofs, beneath the lamp-light; the strong crust
Of friendly bread; and many-tasting food;
Rainbows; and the blue bitter smoke of wood;
And radiant raindrops couching in cool flowers;
And flowers themselves, that sway through sunny hours,
Dreaming of moths that drink them under the moon;
Then, the cool kindliness of sheets, that soon
Smooth away trouble; and the rough male kiss
Of blankets; grainy wood; live hair that is
Shining and free; blue-massing clouds; the keen
Unpassioned beauty of a great machine;
The benison of hot water; furs to touch;
The good smell of old clothes; and other such—
The comfortable smell of friendly fingers,

> *Hair's fragrance, and the musty reek that lingers*
> *About dead leaves and last year's ferns. . . .*
>
> *Dear names,*
> *And thousand others throng to me! Royal flames;*
> *Sweet water's dimpling laugh from tap or spring;*
> *Holes in the ground; and the voices that do sing:*
> *Voices in laughter, too, and body's pain,*
> *Soon turned to peace; and the deep-panting train;*
> *Firm sands; the little dulling edge of foam*
> *That browns and dwindles as the wave goes home;*
> *And washen stone, gay for an hour; the cold*
> *Graveness of iron; moist black earthen mould;*
> *Sleep; and high places; footprints in the dew;*
> *And oaks; and brown horse-chestnuts, glossy new;*
> *And new-peeled sticks; and shining pools on grass—*
> *All these have been my loves.*

Brooke's list of the things he loved always sets my mind turning with the things I have loved—objects and aspects of the material world. Once I put pen to paper and the following flowed from my unconscious. It's an exercise you might try yourself.

> *Sun on my face in winter. Slanting sunlight late on a summer's afternoon. A spring sunset in pastel shades of red, yellow, and green.*
> *Sunday's mood of quiet. The warm aromas of church full of people in silent meditation.*

A thick weekend newspaper. Books. The magic of words that convey a new idea. Poems that sing of universal experiences. Phrases that cannot be forgotten.

Good, strong coffee. Buttered toast. Oranges that spurt tiny drops of oil when peeled. The tartness of lemons . . . and limes, too.

Flower gardens. Darting butterflies. A hummingbird in midair seemingly motionless, its wings a blur.

A tumble of kittens. The fierce dignity of a cat stalking its prey. The faraway gaze of a zoo tiger.

Mountains capped with snow. Icicles dripping, the drop at the very tip refracting a little world. The first smell of spring in winter. A green shoot piercing mud crusted with frost.

Trillium above a carpet of brown leaves. The solitary caw of a crow. Wind moaning through evergreens. The incense of cedar.

Weathered wood—silver and deeply grained. The way that wood peels when shaved with a plane.

Steps worn from many feet. The solidity and spring of the earth to footsteps. Tree-tunneled country roads.

A small town with one main street. Cafes in the morning.

Visionaries have always allowed the love of things because the love of things eventually leads beyond the things to converge in an overarching meaning. Emerson once noted that materialism always becomes idealism.

Baruch Spinoza reasoned, "Except God, no substance can

be granted or conceived. Whatever is, is in God, and nothing can exist or be conceived without God."

Martin Buber counseled, "Do not be vexed at your delight in creatures and things. But do not let it shackle itself to creatures and things; through these, press on to God."

William Blake cut to the quick: "[W]ho sees the infinite in all things, sees God."

If it's a person whom you want to forgive, place a photograph or other reminder of that person on your altar. Light a single candle to signify your dedication to forgiving. You might write the hurt or indignation you still carry on a small piece of paper and place it in an ashtray or similar dish. At the conclusion of the devotion lift the paper to the flame and let go of what you've been holding as the paper burns to cool ashes.

The days of harvest—ripe and colorful—make me generous of spirit. I find it easier to forgive who or what has offended, burdened, or hurt me. When I do forgive, it seems right. I muse at the perversity—the self-defeating strategy—of holding a grudge or harboring a hurt.

The best expression I know of the grace of forgiveness is a well-known Zen parable.

Two monks are traveling through the countryside in the muddy season. In the morning, passing through a village they come upon a beautifully dressed woman—a prostitute perhaps—at the side of the road. She wishes to cross the road but obviously doesn't want to soil her dress or shoes by dragging them through the mud.

Instinctively the first monk surmised the situation and walked to her. Putting her upon his back, he carried her across the mud to the other side of the road.

The two monks continued on their journey. At night when they stopped and—according to their vows—were permitted to talk to one another, the second monk exploded. He'd waited hours to admonish his fellow monk. "How, how could you? How could you have carried that woman on your back? Our vows tell us not to consort with women!"

The first monk simply replied, "Oh, her. Are you still carrying her? I left her on the other side of the road hours ago."

This parable has several layers of meaning. One involves forgiveness by providing a lesson of the caustic effect of not forgiving—of holding anger. The damage done is not to the object of the anger, but to the person who harbors the anger inside.

A second and valuable lesson involves subjectivity. Often what we choose to hold on to and not forgive is a misperception or shortcoming on our part. In this parable the second monk has an overly scrupulousness of what his vows are about. The first monk is clearly not guilty of what Emerson called a "foolish consistency," but in helping the woman across the road acted on a higher principle.

What is it that you've been carrying, that you should

have left back on the side of the road? And what effect has
worked on you because you haven't let go?

The spare words of a colleague, Greta W. Crosby, remind me
that forgiveness is a lot like grief. In order to get on with Life,
leave the hurt in the past.

> *Forgiving is not forgetting.*
> *"Forgiveness" is one word but not one act alone.*
> *Forgiveness is the process we live through in order to re-*
> *store a relationship.*
> *Forgiveness is the process of coming back together again*
> *with another or with oneself after a separation based on*
> *wrongdoing or grievous shortcoming.*
> *Sometimes the wrongdoing is the separation.*
> *Forgiveness involves the acknowledgment and, where pos-*
> *sible, the mutual recognition of what went wrong, of what*
> *we are doing to right the balance, and especially of the mean-*
> *ing and importance of the relationship.*
> *Forgiving is not forgetting.*
> *Forgiving is anchoring a wrong in its own time, letting it*
> *recede into the past as we live and move toward the future.*

Jesus' famous prayer, the "Lord's Prayer," makes forgiveness
a variation on the Golden Rule. Just as we don't want grudges
held against us, we shouldn't hold grudges. In the art of politics
this is known as *quid pro quo*, something for something. How
can you expect to be forgiven, if you're not forgiving?

When Time Has Its Way

In the last weeks of summer you can usually find leaves that have begun to change color—green washed in red or yellow. Gather a few of those leaves and arrange them on your altar around a glass votive.

I never want summer to end—not the leisure and not the weather. But it does end. I must return to a regular work routine. Shorter days and a gradual cooling foreshadow summer's counterpoise: winter. I remind myself that this is not only the way things are, but also that every end marks a beginning.

PASSAGE

*The last days of summer
dissolve into time
Like the morning mist
dissolves in the sun
of a new day.*

*There is a gentle sadness
over the passing of summer.*

There is always sadness
Whenever
a season, era, or life
is ending.

But the passing
Brings a new season—
And with that new season
hope, freshness, and vigor.
The new season's promise
will not be denied
by the melancholy
of that which is ending
or has already dissolved.

Rather than being saddened
by the passing,
Be invigorated
by the hope, freshness, vigor,
And, yes, promise
of the new season that beckons.

In its own way,
Each season will be
as good,
As the season before
And the season to come.

I like Judith Viorst's term for the chain of transitions in a human Life: necessary losses. Just as the end of summer is predictable, so the losses of our lives are predictable. They follow an order. To grow, to mature, and to acquire wisdom in our individual lives we must give up what's become familiar and comfortable, sometimes when it seems we've just settled in. We dredge up our resolve, we take a risk again and again because we reasonably know that everything will work out all right—eventually. We grieve a little and move on, or sometimes we grieve a lot and stall when the loss is great. Yet even the deepest grief will lessen in time; and we rise to a new beginning.

Isn't it curious, when we've entered a new stage, the events of the preceding stages take on a new reality? We realize that the only way to keep is to let go.

WHEN TIME HAS ITS WAY

Day spills from day.
Seasons cycle.
Years accumulate.
Nothing endures unchanged
when time has its way.

But beneath the changes,
indeed, within the changes,
There is the constancy
of continuity:
Spilling days,

Edward Searl

Cycling seasons,
Accumulating years.

No moment, no thought, no action, no life
is ever lost—really.
Each endures in what is and will be
as the parent endures in the child.

Know that you are a part
of all that you have met
and have touched—
Not in mere nostalgia. No!
Rather in the ceaseless unfolding of events
through time into eternity.

Cherish what you have begotten
even as you
Cherish your own fleeting life.

autumn

No other seasonal altar offers so many possibilities. Cattails, milkweed pods, colored leaves, ears of corn, apples, pears, persimmons, pumpkins, concord grapes, chrysanthemums and other autumnal flowers leap to mind. I think the most meaningful objects are those found out of doors—these are the things that speak most strongly to you. Create an evocative autumn tableau from things you find on a walk. I pick what I call a vagabond's bouquet of goldenrod and purple asters along a roadside for my autumn altar. Light a spicy scented column candle to remind you of the pleasant days of domesticity to come when the weather cools.

First and foremost I'm an autumn person. I love autumn's images, sensations, and moods. The most poignant of seasons, autumn reflects the two faces of spirituality. "The scarlet autumn stands for vigorous activity; the gray autumn for meditative feeling," Henri Amiel wrote. I agree. Autumn brings out the poet *and* the priest in me.

My esthetic, poetic side revels in glorious September and October days.

Edward Searl

EARLY AUTUMN

Reds and yellows
in random splashes
on green foliage;
Cloud-cover and sunshine—
days of gray and of clarity;
Equal hours of night and day:
Counterpoise—a season of balance,
When change seems momentarily
suspended.
The many sensations are strong,
because not one overwhelms.

Before the darkness,
Before the cold,
Before the gloom
Of winter begin to congeal,
Feel the balance,
Be suspended on the edge
of change,
Experience equally
the many sensations,
Overcome alienation,
And reestablish
your relationship
with the sacred order
of the earth.

The priest in me begins to stir when October edges toward November. I become deeply meditative.

A DEEPER REALITY

When skies darken
and the temperature drops,
When fallen leaves
swirl in brown eddies,
When bare branches
shiver in the wind,
When hard, cold rain
spatters window panes—
Thoughts become pensive.
We luxuriate
in the warmth of home
and the glow of companions.
Our range of senses
are keen and penetrating.

Is it only instincts stirred?
Are we merely creatures of the earth
remembering we must
prepare for winter?

Or is it a deeper reality
at work?
A religious awareness

that only autumn's darker
and colder moods can bring?

Late autumn penetrates—
body, mind,
and spirit, too—
All that makes soul.

We need a full and balanced awareness of Life and how an individual being fits into Life. Autumn offers varied blessings that together reveal the roundness of Life.

AUTUMN BLESSINGS

I wish for you many autumn blessings:
Many visions to store away: swirling flocks of birds; vivid colors and smoky horizons; stands of cattails; white clouds sculling across blue skies; brown fields of corn; windrows of leaves.
Crystalline days and inky nights.
The acrid aroma of leaf smoke, stirring memory.
A cleansing wind in your hair and clothes.
The friendly warmth of wool and the reassuring sound of your furnace firing for the first time.
The mystery of geese calling in the night.
An apple you have picked—tart and sweet, crisp and hefty, with cool white flesh and waxy sun-warmed skin—to bring a keen sense of Life's proportionate ambiguity.

A bouquet of mums in a sun-drenched window and the bare asymmetry of branches splayed against a gray sky.

The good toil and rich aromas of leaf-raking.

An increasing domesticity, especially the evening companionship of family and friends.

Long shadows and the rare tranquility of early evening— after the leaves have fallen.

Tentative, first flakes of snow.

A private harvest and a heartfelt Thanksgiving for Life's purpose and order.

Is there any season better suited to experience Life's contrasts?

Yes, autumn blessings for you in these days of sharp contrasts.

You may be saying good-bye to your young child who's gone off to kindergarten or first grade, or perhaps one who's going off to college. Place that child's photograph on your altar. Maybe you're saying good-bye to a wonderful summer or some other phase of your own life. Find a way of representing what has ended. You might need to say good-bye to someone who has died. Place a photo or memento of that person on your altar. Light a single candle to begin this devotion. When the devotion has ended blow out the candle with mindfulness that you must let go.

This devotion suits any season of the year. In particular, autumn's events and moods evoke a range of good-byes.

We're always saying good-bye—lots of little good-byes and occasional big ones. The little good-byes come so easily we hardly know we're offering them.

The big good-byes come harder: When we send a child off to school for the first time. When we leave a familiar place to begin anew somewhere else. When a relationship or marriage ends. When a person we love dies. Then the word is hard to say, constricting our throat with emotion.

We can't leave another person without acknowledgment. Good-bye acknowledges that something of value is being given up, if only temporarily.

Good-bye comes with its own gesture—a gesture that may be, after a smile and peek-a-boo, the earliest nonverbal communication we teach a baby. "Good-bye," we say again and again, waving a cupped hand.

Good-bye contains one of the most powerful messages we utter. It's both a summary and an invocation—a rich blessing.

Ponder its double intention. It's actually a contraction of "God be with you," but as we've come to know it, good-bye conveys the general notion of good: beneficial, agreeable, harmonious, and so much more. One aspect of the word looks back at what was and affirms: It was good! A second aspect looks forward and wishes that the very best will unfold: Let it be good! Good-bye contains a richness of what was and what will be. It reminds us that in order to keep, we must continually let go—that we must have the lightest touch with what and whom we love. That light touch is for ourselves as much as for them.

When we haven't had the chance to say good-bye, especially a big good-bye, our spirit is unsettled until we find a way to send that message.

When we do say good-bye, we can get on with our living.

In this way, good-bye is a self-blessing—a permission to leave the past to the past and move into the future.

There's much left unsaid, but implied, in our good-byes. Let the following give partial expression to what is customarily left unspoken.

UNTIL WE MEET AGAIN

Until we meet again,
May there be gentle moments
and tender mercies,
quietly satisfying and full of peace.
May there be adventure, too,
the thrill and reward of the search
and also of the unexpected.
May there be laughter
to sweeten the bitterness
of any tears.
And may there be love—
love given and received.
Until we meet again.

May we be in one another's
minds and hearts,
In God's hands,
Until we meet again . . .

An Apple Accounting

Place a bowl of shiny red apples on your altar. Arrange a pair of candles on either side of the apples so the candlelight will glow in the apple skins.

I know of no better way to stimulate the Harvest Season's deep sense of gratitude than to make what I call an apple accounting.

Indulge your senses, awaken memory, and stimulate gratitude with an ordinary, humble apple— fresh, waxy, plump, and red. Take one from the bowl. Polish it to a rich glow, in which you can see your reflection. Encounter its natural beauty.

Before taking a wonderful bite, imagine: The March thawing of the fertile earth and the first flow of sap rushing through winter-stiff branches—aching from dormancy and itching for life. The cool showers of April seeping into roots and swelling buds. The May perfume of astonishingly white apple blossoms, blushed with pink—buzzed and kissed by bees. The steady green growth of youthful June. The swelling heat of days and the embrace of heavy nights in July. August's ripening and deepening colors. September's coolness penetrating deep into the flesh, sweetening as it chills. The yellow glow of October's harvest moon waxing the red skin.

Winter melts to spring; spring matures to summer; summer ripens to autumn: the unity of Life from blossom to fruit.

In the intimations of cold and heat, drought and rain, sunshine and darkness, fair weather and storm, envision the roundness of days and the cycles of earth. And hidden deep in the flesh, know that seeds wait to renew life through eternity.

Hold the fruit in your hand, feeling its heft and hardness. Run your fingers over the smoothness of its skin. Smell its sweet, fruity perfume. Once again see your reflection, as though the apple holds you in its meaning even as you hold its meaning in your imagination.

Take a bite. Savor textures and tastes. In the crunch and the juice, in the firmness and yielding of the flesh, in the tartness and sweetness, you know the proportion and the goodness of things. Here is evidence of Nature's beauty, bounty, and order.

Remember your reflection in the apple's skin. Nature has blessed you, too.

Let your personal memory quicken and take an accounting of your own life through your days and seasons—an accounting that brings you the realization of your good fortune to be a living, sensing, feeling, thinking creature.

In this apple you experience firsthand a genuine thanksgiving for the miracle of Life, in the scheme of things so improbable but inevitable; so fragile, yet tenacious, beautiful, and abundant.

Now eat your apple. It is the fruit of the Tree of Life: the Universalist apple of the following playful and joyous meditation by Michael J. Murphy:

Ah, the apple, the Universalist fruit—
Subtle. Happy. Inspiring. Inclusive.
No other fruit compares!

The peach is more meditative, scratching its fuzzy face and pondering its pitted navel. Strawberries are fun, but are impressed with themselves and spoil easily. Pears are gritty, but otherwise boring. Lemons and limes are provocative, but all wrapped up in themselves. Bananas are slapstick, cherries are sexy, grapes are passionate, pumpkins overbearing, and tomatoes confused.

But it is the Universalist Apple that encouraged Eve and Adam to seek knowledge, that knocked Newton on his noggin, that inspired Johnny Appleseed.

Adaptive to cooler climates and rural settings, this flexible fruit inspires songs and poetry, patriotism and motherhood. Hot, cold, solid, saucy or cider, nothing tastes better with cinnamon, powdered doughnuts, vanilla ice cream, melted caramels or nuts.

They juggle, they bob, they crunch, and they keep doctors away. Their spirit brings joy, playfulness, knowledge, and nourishment, with no threats of damnation.

A symbol and gift of our bountiful Mother Earth, the flexible, multitalented, spiritual Universalist Apple.

Select a photograph or print of a tranquil autumn landscape for this altar dedicated to peace. I use a photograph of a river with colored leaves floating on the surface that I took one hushed October morning. I add a fresh bouquet of goldenrod and wild asters. A shallow glass bowl filled with clear water helps me imagine an inner serenity.

I've had many occasions, in many places, when I felt at peace—when my spirit reposed harmoniously. It's happened in cities. It's happened with others. It's happened in winter. But most often it's happened in Nature, alone, often in early autumn.

I remember one late September morning when Creation washed the day in gold. On my way from Montreal to Burlington, I was driving down a ribbon of asphalt on the narrow chain of islands in the upper part of Lake Champlain known as the Heroes. Fog gave the landscape a soft focus. The maples by the side of the road had already colored—some red and orange, most a butterscotch yellow. The occasional houses and barns were dream-like. Then, as though a switch had been thrown, the sun shone through the fog, and every droplet of water turned misty gold. I wanted to be gilded, too.

I stopped the car and walked along the water's edge where a small bridge joined island to island. Little waves lapped the shore and crows cawed. I lingered as the sun burned off the fog. Bright colors emerged from the mist. The rolling contours of farm fields appeared around me. Corn plants heavy with ears reached from where I'd stopped down to the lake. The lake stretched west to the jagged high peaks of the Adirondacks and east to the rounded Green Mountains that folded into one another. The tranquil world was unveiled around me.

My God, that was a beautiful day! But had I been troubled in spirit, I wouldn't have felt the incredible peace that flooded my soul. A stilled mind allowed my soul to repose in the beauty. As a reminder of this state of mind, I wrote a meditation.

BE STILL

Once in a while
Still yourself.
Let your throbbing pulse
calm.
Let your racing thoughts
slacken.

Edward Searl

Let your frantic actions
dissipate.

Find yourself
Not at the accustomed center
of a busy world,
Rather find yourself as one element,
reposing in a complex harmony.

Know the tidal flow of eternity
buoying your being in its rhythms.
Feel the sure cycles of the seasons
stirring in your flesh.

Marvel at the beauty
registering on your senses.
Wonder at the orderliness
of the material world and living things.
Intuit the purpose
greater than, yet including, you.

Still yourself.
Enter into the Universal
Where you will find yourself no stranger.

Later I thought about how, knowing peace myself, I might multiply that peace with other persons and in my world.

PEACE, FRIENDS.

Peace:
let us give
one another
the gifts of peace.

Let there be peace
of mind.
No longer troubled
by self-doubt or guilt,
confident of our ability and worth,
We shall discover inner contentment.

Let there be a deep peace
of the soul,
As we grow in harmony
with the Larger Reality
embracing us.

Let there be peace
among neighbors and nations.
As we seek to end
all acts of hostility and aggression
that defeat and destroy.

Peace, friends.
May we be granted

the gifts of peace,
Friends.

Peace, friends.
May we give
the gifts of peace,
Friends.

Peace, friends.

The Beauty of Imperfection

In imitation of the October tea—of the Japanese tea ceremony—set this altar with a napkin or mat worn from use and many washings, an old tea pot, cup and saucer. Fill the pot with green tea and hot water.

For years I've believed that an utter goodness permeates Creation. In its sum, Creation is perfect. Yet I've become increasingly aware of the existential reality of my own being—my limitations, especially my mortality. I experience the human condition as bittersweet. Through the generations human beings endure, but each generation lives and dies. I strive to accept this reality, to affirm it in faith, and to live my life wisely and bravely in its truth.

G. Peter Fleck, in *The Blessings of Imperfection*, has helped me express my faith:

The only time the world was perfect was before it was created. When it was still but an idea, a glint in the creator's eye. But when it was put together in matter when it materialized it was no longer perfect; it was good. It was as good as possible.

Late October brings to me a visceral realization of the cycles of earthly life—of one generation preparing the way for the next generation. Several years ago I learned of a Japanese esthetic: *wabi* (rhymes with hobby). *Wabi* nearly overwhelms me in late October.

Wabi *speaks to the beauty of impermanence, imperfection, and incompleteness with strong ties to that which is modest, humble, and even unconventional.*

For example, the Japanese would treasure a teacup made by an old tea-master—a teacup with a crack—as much for the crack as for the age and artistic quality of the teacup. The crack is a signature of the cup's creation—a beautiful flaw— that marks the cup's moment of creation and distinguishes it from all other cups.

In the yearly cycle of the tea ceremony, October tea has the most wabi. *Mismatched and lovingly mended dishes are used and the last of the year's tea is used up. The tea drinker savors that which is in the process of expiring.*

Autumn's sweet melancholy registers wabi *on the human soul. Age lines in an elder's face have* wabi. *An old barn worn by weather and the worrying of animals has* wabi. *A threshold worn by the passage of many feet has* wabi.

I think when we see our own self and one another through the lens of wabi, *we learn to accept, even love, what*

once seemed shortcomings, impermanence, and imperfec-
tions.

I've spoken to my congregation about *wabi*, using the preceding illustrations. Many persons found the concept useful and
have let me know that they understood the concept. One incident makes me laugh whenever I think about it. At an afternoon
gathering, while drinking after-dinner coffee from cherished
family china at a friend's house, I knocked my cup and saucer
from a side table and broke both pieces. I felt totally embarrassed. I couldn't fix or replace what I'd broken. A few days later
I received an elaborately wrapped present for my altar: the beautiful antique saucer glued back together and a display stand.

I set my *wabi* altar with that broken and repaired plate.
Because I broke it in a clumsy movement, it reminds me of my
own imperfections. I also set out a pot of hot tea and an old
cup and saucer in imitation of the October tea.

The friend, Melinda Perrin, who made me a gift of the broken saucer, later wrote a poem. This poem is one that has become a favorite affirmation of the beauty of imperfection.

IN PRAISE OF IMPERFECTION

—an ode to middle age—

> *My daughter stands before the mirror*
> *Cheeks sucked in*

Mouth pursed in a bow
Arranging a wayward lock.

"I hate my hair!" she exclaims.
I sigh.
Imperfection is much easier
When you don't have a choice.
That's why I love middle age.

When I was young I worried about:
My weight
My hair
My shape
My derriere.
Now I buy a larger size.

Youth is a time of competition.
The subtle comparison at the beach:
The size of breasts
The muscle tone
The tan
The grace
The curve of hips.
Now I think, "Not bad for an old broad!"
And dig into potato chips.
It's much more fun being middle-aged.

A Place of Your Own

There's a comfort that comes from the well-worn and familiar,
Be it shoes or body or relationships.
When there's love and lovely shared experiences,
Flaws become endearments.
Whether scars, jokes, or scuffs,
It's much easier being middle-aged.

The shift I find is one of attitude,
Of acceptance and love for myself and others.
Our bodies are there to keep us human.
Imperfection is a fact of life,
Something that marks us unique, not factory-made,
A living, breathing part of creation,
All be it of middle age.

Be playful with this altar. Be imaginative in using customary symbols of Halloween. I prefer symbols of the harvest—ears of Indian corn and miniature pumpkins, arranged on brown maple leaves I've gathered off the ground. Try your hand at carving a miniature pumpkin and placing a votive candle in it.

Late afternoon one Halloween, I was driving through a small Ohio town. The sun had dipped toward the horizon in a cloudless sky. Oranges, yellows, and an occasional slash of red still flamed on the old maple trees that lined the streets of Victorian houses. Plenty of leaves had already fallen to lay a shiny brown carpet on the broad front lawns. When the wind blew, leaves skittered on the street. Children, dressed as ghosts, skeletons, and witches, clutched booty bags, and skittered among the houses. They seemed ethereal spirits from an otherworld.

Maybe the effect was heightened by being in a country town with corn shocks tied to its light posts. Maybe it was my state of mind. I felt something very ancient and intuited a wordless reason for what I once dismissed as the child's play of trick or treat.

I've gained respect for the seasonal appropriateness of Halloween. I've got some Celtic blood in me—a quarter Irish and a quarter British via Normandy. My internal calendar seems tuned to the original Celtic year divided into two seasons: summer and winter. Summer began on May 1, or *Beltane*. Winter began on November 1, or *Samhain*.

On *Samhain* the Celts celebrated New Year. They believed that on this New Year's Day the dead returned to the land of the living. The days that surround Samhain were days of chaos when the old year's order had dissolved and the new year's order had not yet gained control. The Celts dressed in costume, played pranks, and made merry. They also believed that the veil between the worlds had grown thin. New Year's Eve, perched between two years, stood outside of time and offered a vantage that favored fortune-telling and divination.

I suspect that our contemporary Halloween remembers these ancient Celtic customs. Why else dress in costumes, play pranks, appease restless spirits with offerings of food, and keep evil spirits at bay with lighted candles? Halloween responds to a mood of Nature in late October. A cycle of the earth has ended and a new cycle has begun. Part and parcel with Nature, our flesh stirs and thoughts and feelings well-up from the depths of our psyches.

I confirm what I realize throughout the year, but which is now especially strong. I belong to the earth. Its rhythms are my rhythms.

OF THE EARTH

We belong to the earth,
Not the earth belongs
to us.
Out of the elements,
Shaped by cycles
of our spinning, journeying planet;
With an inarticulate urge
to always become something new—
We have emerged
And continue emerging.

Conscious and self-conscious,
Knowing and in our knowing,
wondering—
We have emerged
and continue emerging.

In each of us
all the diverse elements,
Every rhythm and cycle
of the faintest pulse
of the dullest bit of matter,
Seeks expression
And moves toward wonder.

And we,
with the power to speak,
Find the deepest expressions
Unspeakable.
Still we persist,
Because we are the earth
Grown conscious.

Because I sense, feel, and intuit more than I can express at this earth-centered New Year, I give this altar special attention.

With that backward and forward vision attributed to the ancient Celtic New Year, I see clearly my relationship to Life—a taking and giving that involves my fellow human beings and all of Nature.

A NATURAL ORDER

The last leaves
cling to the trees.
In a week
They too will fall,
joining the wrinkled mass
already on the ground.
The cool air
carries the rich pungency
of damp leaves decaying
In this way

*That taken from the earth
returns to the earth.*

*The life there was
in a season of green
drew sustenance
from prior season of life,
In return
sustenance will be given
to generations to come.*

*This is the natural order,
the cycle of seasons and living things.*

*Let us learn to take
when we need to take;
Let us learn to give
when others have need.*

*Giving and taking
is the ongoing celebration
of living.
In the celebration
all life is enriched.*

You might be able to find traditional Day of the Dead decorations for this altar—sugar skulls and coffins, paper streamers, a skeleton figure, candleholder, or "bread of the dead"—in a Mexican grocery or shop. Strew yellow chrysanthemum petals on your altar or fashion a bouquet.

Perhaps you want to create an ofrenda *of a particular person. Put a variety of objects, foods, and other things that represent that person for you.*

I n Mexico the first and second of November belong to the dead. Indigenous traditions predating the 1521 Spanish Conquest melded into All Saints and All Souls Days of the conquering Catholic tradition to create the uniquely Mexican festival of *Dia de los Muertos*: The Day of the Dead.

Late October and early November—when leaves have fallen, cold seeps in, and darkness comes early—evoke pensiveness. Earth-centered traditions speak of the curtain between the world of the living and dead growing thin and tearing at this time of year, through which the spirits return to the earth. Halloween marks the ancient Celtic New Year's holiday of *Samhain*.

The Day of the Dead, poised on the far side of the warm season from the relatively brighter and gayer Memorial Day, offers a frank way of dealing with mortality and death by exaggeration and excess.

The Day of the Dead mixes carnival and piety. Families keep vigil throughout the night at graves decorated with yellow chrysanthemums, offerings of food, and lighted candles. Artisans sell grimly humorous toys such as *papier-mâche* tableaus of skeleton people and animals—for example, a skeleton bride and groom with the legend "Until Death Do Us Part." Paper streamers depicting symbols of death such as skulls or skeleton dancers hang like bunting. Children eagerly buy decorated sugar skulls and coffins, often inscribed with their names and premature epitaphs, from street vendors. Bakers sell little loaves known as "bread of the dead," sprinkled with colored sugar and sometimes shaped like people.

Yellow chrysanthemum petals strewn on paths treading to the front doors invite spirits of the dearly beloved into homes. House altars, a custom the church didn't condone and could never suppress, adorned with flowers, leaves, vegetables, and fruit, welcome and feed the spirits.

Mexican immigrants to the United States have brought the Day of the Dead with them. The tradition of house altars (*ofrendas*) continues and has grown into the custom of creating public altars.

Artists, seeking to recall and work their tradition in a new environment, have made Day of the Dead altars fantastic public art. Sometimes these altars are dedicated to an individual—a close relative or perhaps a public figure. Sometimes these altars memorialize a group, such as grandparents who emigrated to the United States. Always the altars are decorated with things closely related to that person or group—favorite beverages and food, tools, photographs, any evocative memorabilia or mementos.

There's a paradoxical freedom in Day of the Dead observances—the freedom of indulgence and excess, of creativity and art. They offer serious playfulness. As a yearly observance, a Day of the Dead home altar can be powerful personal therapy for dealing with death and coming to terms with your own mortality as well as the deaths of your beloved. While not for everyone, this early November observance may suit your sensibilities and meet deep needs, synchronizing your personal spirit with Earth's spirit of early November.

DAYS OF MEMORY

These are days of memory.
It has always been so
for our kind
After the leaves have fallen.
The nights are long.
And in the darkness
We remember.

These are days of reflection.
the long, horizontal rays
of the thin afternoon sun
Spill across the earth
with the golden light of memory.

A chilling breeze at twilight
Stirs the ground cover of leaves,
Stirring also our thoughts.

The elusive beauty of red sunsets
We would hold,
if only we could.
But darkness seeps
from below the horizon.
Day turns into dusk into night.

So, we remember.
In our minds,
In the golden light of memory,
We affirm the eternal beauty
of the lives of those who have died
and the goodness of the days that were.

These are days of memory,
of reflection,
of affirmation.
It has always been so for our kind,
After the leaves have fallen.

Week 47

Home

Let the altar you dedicate to your home and its spiritual possibilities express beauty. You don't need to signify or represent the notion of home, because you're in the midst of it. Give special, loving care to arrange a beautiful bouquet—a tangible symbol of the larger care you take to have a "house beautiful."

At-homeness is a spiritual condition. It is a signature of a grounded and congruent personal spirituality. It means being at home with your own self, with your fellow human beings, with Nature, with the Divine.

Today, we're relearning how important our individual homes are—the places where each of us lives. Your home gives you comfort, refreshment, and meaning found nowhere else. In this regard, our homes are refuges; and they are also places of ultimate creation—where we create our *self* even as we create the place called *home*. Self and home entwine.

Perhaps you haven't discovered the nuturing possibilities of your home. You need to repose in your home to appreciate how you've made it your own and how it reflects complexities and nuances of your life. The following reflection composed by Ellie Searl can guide you in how you might encourage your own sense of *at-homeness*.

AT HOME

I never used to want to rise earlier than the sun, but lately I've begun to savor the wee first hours of each day. While I wait for a crack in the almost-morning sky, I imagine every place, every corner, and every treasure of my home. Memory treasures. Treasures our family has gathered through the years of living. Chairs and tables, vases and pictures. Sculptures and coats, lap throws and newspapers. All of these in comforting disarray of living. We fill the rooms of our lives with love and bustle and happiness. My home is alive with the stories and the memories made by the people that matter most to me.

In the quiet of dawn, I sit in my familiar morning place and absorb the sweetness of home. I'm surrounded by adventures of family, togetherness and time, and I can play the stories over and over again. Across the room, on an unfolded afghan throw, lies last Sunday's jointly completed puns and anagrams puzzle. I laugh at my competitiveness, and vow to share next time. Beside it is the broken-spined dictionary that ended one of our word scuffles. My coffee cup rests on the old blanket chest we bought so many years ago on a trip through the Canadian Rockies, the day we celebrated our daughter's 8th birthday around a pine forest campfire. We'd *made s'mores with leathery marshmallows, and her favorite present was a ballpoint pen with a floating canoe in the pen top. My feet curl up on the couch that fills my mind with endless walks through city department stores and furniture shops looking for just the right one with lots of pillows and a high snuggle factor. The living room walls hold miniature seasonal photographs taken by my husband during a year's worth of daily afternoon bicycle rides. In one picture, the mist hovers over newly budded trees beside a spring river, and the pebbles reflect upside down in the smooth, flooded banks of the park. I had biked with him that day, and we drank hot coffee with our gloves on because of the early spring chill. I look at the old, upright piano that we bought for $50 when we had so little to spare. I can't bring myself to give the piano away, even though I've promised to at least a hundred times. Too many hours stripping off the black stain to uncover the gleaming mahogany, and too many piano lessons keep my piano cemented in my home of stories.*

The sun streams into the room and makes lacy patterns on the floor. I remember that today is beginning. I'm energized; I feel the surge of newness and the possibilities of creating. I'll take the blessings of my home with me as I go through the day. And later, in the evening, I'll watch the sun set on new memories captured by the spirit of home.

The notion of *home* involves a sense of belonging so intimate that your being seeps into your home. William Channing Gannett in his influential late–nineteenth-century essay "House

Beautiful" realized that a home isn't merely a physical building and collection of objects. It's those material things infused with ideals and spirit and humanity. I love Gannett's phrase to describe this transcendental process: "domestication of the infinite."

FROM HOUSE BEAUTIFUL

How much more than house is Home! Cellar and walls and roof, chairs and tables and spoons—these are the mere shell of the Home. . . .

And still one thing remains to furnish the House Beautiful, the most important thing of all, without which guests and books and flowers and pictures and harmonies of color only emphasize the fact that the house is not a home. I mean the warm light in the rooms that comes from kind eyes, from quick unconscious smiles, from gentleness in tones, from little unpremeditated caresses of manner, from habits of thoughtfulness for one another—all that happy illumination which, on the inside of a house, corresponds to morning sunlight outside falling on quiet dewy fields.

Louis Untermeyer, in his poem "Prayer for a New House," expressed my intentions for you—that "every casual corner blooms into a shrine." I wish you a house that is a home altar—a spiritual place of your own.

PRAYER FOR A NEW HOUSE

May nothing evil cross this door,
And may ill-fortune never pry
About these windows; may the roar
And rains go by.

Strengthened by faith, these rafters will
Withstand the battering of the storm;
This hearth, though all the world grow
chill,
Will keep us warm.

Peace shall walk softly through these
rooms,
Touching our lips with holy wine,
Till every casual corner blooms
Into a Shrine.

Laughter shall drown the raucous shout;
And, though these sheltering walls are
thin,
May they be strong to keep hate out
And hold love in.

This devotion suggests a wealth of settings. Don't rely on the well-worn, familiar. Find personal representations and symbols of those things for which you're most grateful. Make it as beautiful as you can—colorful, textured, varied, even resplendent with the aromas of ripe fruit and burning candles.

The word *thanks* has its origin in a Latin word meaning to *know* and a subsequent Old English word meaning *thought*. It makes sense to me that *thought* and *knowledge* precede a heartfelt giving of thanks.

I've collected dozens of Thanksgiving litanies—accountings of gratitude. The following, adapted from a turn of the century hymnal is a favorite. I love its beauty of expression and breadth of vision.

"ALL THE GLADNESS OF LIFE"

For the Gift of Life in this wonderful world; for the miracle and high cost of its making; for health, and the joy of the body; for the mind, for conscience, for soul ever seeking to see and know:

In mindful thanksgiving, lift a glad song of wonder and praise.

For the changing Seasons and the beautiful Face of the Year. For the splendor of Winter days and nights; for the starry hosts of the storm, and the sparkling silence of snow-clad fields:

In mindful thanksgiving, lift a glad song of wonder and praise.

For the coming of Spring; for the rebirth of Life, and all the flowering things; for running brooks, and budding woods, and birdsong in the trees:

In mindful thanksgiving, lift a glad song of wonder and praise.

For the joyous hours of Summer rest; for the vision of beauty on every side—the glory of hills and the sea and the wide green earth, of sunset and twilight and star-lit nights:

In mindful thanksgiving, lift a glad song of wonder and praise.

For bountiful Autumn; for the red and gold of the woodlands; for the wheat and corn and the ripened fruits, and the merry-makings of harvest-home:

In mindful thanksgiving, lift a glad song of wonder and praise.

For honorable and disciplined ancestry; for the joys of Home, and the daily communion of gladness and sorrow; for the strong heart and strong arm of the father; for the gentleness of mothers; for the laughter and music of children:

In mindful thanksgiving, lift a glad song of wonder and praise.

For all Leaders—searchers of Nature, thinkers, inventors and public servants; artists and poets and prophets of truth; defenders of freedom and justice, martyrs and saints; and for the multitude, humble and faithful, unthanked and unknown lovers of humanity.

In mindful thanksgiving, lift a glad song of wonder and praise.

For Righteousness at the heart of the world; for evil turned into good and sorrow to joy; for darkness giving way to the sunshine; for truth victorious over injustice—no good thing, a failure—no evil, success; for faith in humanity, in progress, in Goodness Eternal, for all the Gladness of Life in this wonderful world, and the heart's assurance of Life that endures through the generations.

In mindful thanksgiving, lift a glad song of wonder and praise.

I find Thanksgiving the purest of our contemporary holidays—a harvest festival enjoyed at home, with food and the company of family and friends. Thanksgiving takes holy pause from most of the commercialism and materialism that surround other holidays. In that holy pause we think and know the gifts of Life, the graces and tender mercies of our fellow women and men. We also enjoy particular pleasures, pleasures that shape this beloved day.

THANKSGIVING BLESSINGS

I wish you Thanksgiving blessings:

A gathering of family and friends around the table.

Savory aromas of baking and cooking—turkey and bread, steaming vegetables and spicy pies.

Cranberry sauce the way you like it; perhaps jellied and from a can.

A generous portion of pumpkin pie with a dollop of real whipped cream please, no dairy substitute.

After dinner, whatever your pleasure may be—conversation, football on the TV, a walk in the slanting sun of late afternoon, or a nap.

The first flush of excitement and wonder of the Holidays— before the flush becomes a fever.

A bedtime snack of savory leftovers.

A peaceful day and, nestled in the peace, a mystical moment, when you realize the goodness of Life and its generous abundance for you.

Thanksgiving blessings to you.

Last week your altar may have overflowed in gratitude for Life's bounty. This altar offers a sharp contrast. Find a photograph or print in which you can see through bare trees to a far horizon. A solitary taper, its flame moving to the slightest current of air, adds to the sense of solitude and contemplation.

Thanksgiving has ended. I haven't begun holiday preparations yet. The towering stack of Christmas catalogs arriving in the mail remains deliberately unread.

I save the end of November, the beginning of December as treasured holy days—a holiday of Solitude. (*Holiday*, remember, is a form of *holy day*.) I need to walk outdoors, to find patches of leafless woods, and to let my vision rest on far horizons. The quality of sunlight—thin and slanting—can bring me to tears of wordless emotion.

LUCID, DEEP, AND PENETRATING

After the leaves have fallen,
When trees are laid bare;

A Place of Your Own

> Before the first snowfall
> Blankets the earth,
> There are a few rare weeks
> of clear skies;
>
> When sunlight
> bounces, reflects, illuminates
> As it could not
> Before.
> Then,
> Just now,
> in the turning of the Seasons,
> Our vision becomes—
> suddenly, exceptionally—
> lucid, deep, and penetrating.
>
> Now is the time
> To see what was hidden;
> To see to the horizon;
> To see a revelation too poignant for words.
>
> To you,
> Just now,
> The opportunity and wisdom
> to discover
> Nature's revelation
> Between the falling of the leaves
> and the falling of the snow.

To you,
Just now,
A time to see and know
As it was not possible
Until now.

Solitude isn't deprivation. It's leanness in Nature, in my life, in my senses. I see more clearly now, as I'm forced to look at what's been hidden in Nature, in other persons, in myself. *Clear sight* I call it. I can make sense of what had been confused.

No one wants a life of unbroken solitude, a life entirely alone and probably lonely. Solitude is a spiritual retreat. If you feel lonely when you try it, you're missing the meaning of solitude. Solitude involves relationships stripped down to their essentials—face-to-face, frank and honest. Solitude calibrates your conscious mind and your soul.

The best writers I know on solitude are women: May Sarton who wrote a *Journal of Solitude* and even better, Doris Grumbach, who in her elder years explored *Fifty Days of Solitude* in the midst of a bleak Maine winter. Generally more relational than men, women often face solitude with dread of the unknown that includes encountering their deep self—possibly for the first time. Always the insights of solitude cluster around a stark honesty.

A PRECARIOUS BALANCE

Weigh your spiritual health
on a balance.

A Place of Your Own

On one side
Heap on your need to be alone,
Your yearning to retreat inward
to silence and solitude.
Pile on your selfish desires
and your self-seeking ways.
(Do not be embarrassed by them,
they are important and real.)
Unload your weighty ego here.

On the other side
Heap on your compassion and concern.
Your love for your fellow kind
leading you outward.
Pile on your instincts
to find companions of heart and mind.
Gently lay here your selflessness,
your willingness to give,
even sacrifice yourself,
for another person or cause.
Here is room for your conscience;
treat it gently.

Never stop heaping as long as you live.
On either side the piles will grow
The balance will be unsteady,

tipping from one side to the other,
tipping between selfishness and selflessness.
Always seek a steady level,
a precarious balance.
The art of living is to somehow
keep the balance of Life
throughout the shifting changes.

This seasonal interlude in Nature and in human affairs suits itself to solitude that finds a balance of Life in your life.

I suggest two possibilities for your Tree of Life altar. The first is arty. Select a branch that when placed in a vase looks like a small, bare tree. Decorate it with small paper cutouts that represent persons, things, and aspects of your life you cherish. Or, since the holiday season begins after Thanksgiving, place a small traditional evergreen on your altar. Decorate it with tiny lights and small ornaments, or cutouts.

Nothing haunts me more than a winter tree silhouetted against the sky. I stare at the asymmetrical branches and try to grasp the tree's symmetry. The tree's compelling example often grasps me instead.

A tree strikes a balance between heaven and earth: The roots spread nearly as wide and deep as its branches spread wide and high. I want to be down-to-earth *and* spiritual. A tree follows the cycle of seasons, each season marked by a new ring of growth. I want to grow by maturing through the stages of my life. A tree takes nutrients from the soil

and returns oxygen to the atmosphere. I want to give as much
as I take—in harmony with and a blessing to my world.

BETWEEN

Trees respond to sun and earth
and thrive.
Leaves reach for sunlight.
Roots stretch for gravity.
In between heart wood expands.

A tree is a balance
in harmony
with the forces that pull at it.

Contemplate the tree:
see its roots, its heart wood, its leaves;
understand the pulls of earth and sun;
appreciate the flow of sap, the expansion
of heart wood.
For this is what lies
between heaven and earth.

The tree is a universal religious symbol. In Norse mythology
Odin, while tied to the World Tree, gained the knowledge of
language. Adam and Eve ate the fruit of the Tree of Knowledge
but were driven out of paradise so they wouldn't eat of the Tree

of Life and become like God. The cross upon which Jesus died, some contend, is yet another example of the mythic Tree standing at the axis of the World. Saint Boniface, who brought Christianity to Germany, cut down Odin's sacred oak and erected an evergreen tree dedicated to Jesus in its place. From Germany came the custom of the Christmas Tree—one of the most resplendent and accessible examples of the World Tree and Tree of Life.

TWO TREES

In paradise,
so the myth relates,
There were two trees:
The Tree of the Knowledge
of Good and Evil
And the Tree of Life.

Eating of the fruit
of the first tree
Primal man and primal woman
became like God
and the heavenly court,
And lest they eat
of the fruit
of the second tree
And live forever,

And be as God
and the heavenly throng . . .

So, paradise was not lost
But denied. Yet how much
we gained.

Instead of mindless eternity
for you and me
There is knowledge:
Consciousness and self-consciousness;
An awareness of good and evil;
The possibility of wisdom.

In this most ancient myth
an implication:
Beyond knowledge
There is the divine.
The divine is ours
If, in knowledge,
We seek the Tree of Life
And eat of its fruit.

A decade ago I worked with a group, each of us making an individual panel to be included in a great Ribbon of Peace to wind around the Pentagon in Washington, D.C. After much thinking, I decided to make my panel a Tree of Life—a sprawling, bare branched, oak tree. On the branches I placed symbols of the people and things I loved the most, as well as experiences and aspects of my life: a red cardinal for Nature, a daisy for my wife, a teddy bear for my daughter, a square church for my profession, a candle for truth. Brightly colored felt covered all the branches. It was beautiful; but even more, it made me aware of my reverence for my life, rich with people, experiences, and passions.

SYMBOLS OF THE SEASON

The candle,
The evergreen,
The infant child:
These are the symbols of the season.

For we affirm that
a flame
banishes the dreariest darkness.
For we affirm that
the Tree of Life
endures the harshest time.
For we affirm that
the spirit of love
is renewed with the birth of every child.

So it is Light and Life and Love
We see
in the Christmas candle

and in the Christmas tree
and in the Christmas child.

And it is Light and Life and Love
We celebrate.

Leave your altar empty for this devotion. Don't even light a candle.

I know a Chicago church of the liberal tradition—neo-Gothic in design and replete with religious references and symbols—that has on the chancel wall, behind and above the altar, a niche so empty, it echoes silence. It's a deliberate symbol—one of the most compelling religious symbols I've ever encountered. The empty niche provokes me.

My reactions to it vary, depending on my mood. Sometimes I find it restful, as though I've turned off the visual equivalent of loud and distressing music. Sometimes the emptiness strikes me as an absence. Have I been forsaken? Or does it imply that it's up to me to make or find the meaning? Sometimes it seems an invitation to enter emptiness, to explore an unknown realm. I must trust the emptiness. Sometimes it seems a nonverbal Zen *koan*. Understanding, I speculate, if it comes, will be instant enlightenment.

Occasionally I deliberately leave my altar empty.

I have reactions to my empty altar similar to those I have to the empty niche in the Chicago church. This empty altar devotion also makes me more appreciative of the altars I set with objects. An empty altar is an appropriate setting to contemplate the coming of winter. In the cycle of the seasons winter is a stark time that most challenges us.

As I look down the corridor of time, I invoke a religious response to be found in rest and absence—the "pregnant negativities" unique to winter.

SPIRIT OF THE VOID

Spirit of the Void,
Always silent
And never demanding,

Be with me
And in me.
Take me once in a while,
Into Nothingness.

Once in a while,
When my thoughts
Turn too madly
And form too rapidly—
Take me into Nothingness.

A Place of Your Own

Once in a while,
When my home
Is too cluttered with noise
And too crowded with things—
Take me into Nothingness.

Once in a while,
When my day
Is too full of people
And too busy with tasks—
Take me into Nothingness.

Once in a while,
When my world
Is too large in circumference
And its demands too heavy,
Take me into nothingness.

Spirit of the Void,
Take me
Once in a while
Into Nothingness—
So I may
Think more clearly
And rest more peacefully,
And work more productively,
And live more gladly,
When I return.

A Journey to Your Wise Elder

You may have an actual wise elder in your life. Put that person's photograph on your altar. Or find a photograph of an older person whose face strikes you as especially handsome—not in spite of, but because of wrinkled skin and gray hair—the sort of face that seems content and hints at a very wise person who has lived Life fully.

In the psychology of Carl Jung, the wise elder represents the latent wisdom within your psyche and toward which you may grow and become. When you encounter an older person—an actual individual, in your dreams, or through the active imagination of fiction—who strikes you as benevolent and wise, you've met your wise elder. The qualities you admire in that wise elder are your own qualities, realized through a process known as projection.

The following guided meditation will take you to your wise elder—an integral aspect of your own psyche. This is an exercise in going home to the person you may one day be.

A Place of Your Own

PREPARATION

Sit easily in a chair. Your feet rest upon the floor. Your hands are comfortable and your arms relaxed. You are aware of your physical being.

Breathe in. Air fills your lungs. Hold the Breath of Life for a long moment of awareness. Slowly exhale.

Repeat this gentle exercise of breathing and exhaling as you find a center of Self that is surely and essentially you. At that center there is calm—such a calm that your inner eye sees and your inner senses are keen and attentive. Though calm, you are fully alert and responsive. There is no anxiety, no regret, no expectation to disturb the bed of tranquility where you repose with an inner harmony.

You have found a deeper region of the Self: a region beyond your ordinary surface existence. It is familiar, wonderfully real, more essentially you. You are welcome and have a sense of coming home.

Delight in this inner place.

A JOURNEY

You are going on a journey now. You are expectant, but not anxious. You have a destination, but you will not hurry the journey to get there. The journey itself is rewarding and pleasurable.

It is autumn, mid-afternoon. The sky is clear, the air bracing. The golden sun is warm. With the sun blessing your face, you breathe in deep draughts of invigorating air. The sensations are wonderful. They stimulate your inner being, as well as your outer being. You are charged with energy.

You travel country roads that climb and turn—gently. Along the roadside purple asters and goldenrod cluster. There trees are yellow, orange, and red. A few leaves float dreamily through the air before adding to puddles of color on ragged grass. The colors of autumn on the rolling landscape are restful, like a cozy blanket. An occasional field of corn appears, dun brown. Heavy ears bend from the many stalks. You travel for many soothing miles through this countryside. The scenery is a pleasant patchwork repeating hypnotically an inner vision of abundant harvest.

The road you've been traveling joins a small river and follows its bending course. The water carries fallen leaves, reflects the rich colors of the trees, and sky. A slanting sun dapples the water's surface with gilt. The river's course is serpentine; that's okay, because you're in no hurry.

The sun is setting. Dusk descends. The last long golden rays spill almost horizontally, illuminating tree trunks and the lighter underside of the colored leaves. Flocks of birds swirl in the sky one final time before roosting for the night. The light of a village—your destination—beckons a welcome.

It is a village of modest cottages and occasional Victorian houses, wrapped in great porches. Tree-lined streets hold a secret about the rhythms of domesticity. A slight breeze sends dry leaves skittering.

In the midst of the village your destination awaits. You have seen it with your inner eye from the moment you left your own home. It is an old, but well-kept house with a wide porch on three sides. The glow of lights calls you to enter. Someone waits for you—someone who is familiar. The smell of wood smoke is incense purifying and sanctifying all.

YOUR WISE ELDER

Before a fire, sitting serenely in a comfortable armchair is your Wise Elder, waiting patiently for you. You needn't knock, just walk through the great front doors, past the front parlor into the sitting room. It is warm with aromas like a cedar trunk. Your Wise Elder looks up and smiles.

Notice how your Elder appears: aged but firm, serene, and loving. Study the Elder's face rich with fulfillment that comes from living. Look at the hands that have done a lifetime of work—folded in rest.

Your Wise Elder wants to answer your most important questions. Talk to your Wise Elder and let your Wise Elder talk to you. You don't need to hurry or hoard the sensations of your visit. You can return again and again, whenever you need counsel or a comforting peace that can come after the activity and busyness of your day has faded away. Each day your journey to your Wise Elder is a little shorter.

Your Wise Elder is always available to listen, to offer understanding, to speak the wisdom that you know is right as soon as the words are formed.

And knowing this, you say good-bye, embracing your Wise Elder who walks with you to the front door and waits to watch you leave.

As you step outside into the night, you have never felt more composed, more congruent, never more clear-visioned. It's as though your Wise Elder sits alongside you as you resume your journey home. Your breathing is strong and measured.

Breathe in. Breathe out.

Breathe in. Breathe out.

Breathe in. Breathe out.

Until you have returned to this day, this place, and have opened your eyes—glad to have taken a journey to meet your Wise Elder who is always within you.

sources and permissions

We gratefully acknowledge the following publishers and authors who have granted us permission to publish excerpts from their works. Every reasonable effort has been made to obtain appropriate permission to reprint material.

Carlisle, Thomas John. "Our Jeopardy." Published in *Theology Today*, January 1987, vol. XLIII, no.4, p.559. Permission granted by *Theology Today*.

Coots, Max. "Let Us Give Thanks" from *View from a Tree*. Copyright © 1989 by Max Coots. Permission granted by Max Coots.

———. "It's the Little Deaths" from *Seasons of the Self*. Abingdon Press, Nashville, TN. Copyright © 1971 by Abingdon Press. Permission granted by Max Coots.

Crosby, Greta W. "Forgiveness" from *Tree and Jubilee*. Published by the Unitarian Universalist Association, Boston, MA. Copyright © 1982 by the Unitarian Universalist Association. Permission granted by Greta W. Crosby.

————. "Winter" from *Tree and Jubilee*. Published by the Unitarian Universalist Association, Boston, MA. Copyright © 1982 by the Unitarian Universalist Association. Permission granted by Greta W. Crosby.

Foote, Arthur. "Most of Us Dread" from *Taking Down the Defenses*. Published for Unity Church, St. Paul, MN, by Essex Publishing Co., Essex Junction, VT. Copyright © 1972 by Arthur Foote. Permission granted by Arthur Foote.

Murphy, Michael J. *Universalist Apple*. Permission granted by Michael J. Murphy.

Perrin, Melinda. *In Praise of Imperfection*. Permission granted by Melinda Perrin.

Rexroth, Kenneth. From *One Hundred Poems by the Chinese*. Copyright © 1971 by Kenneth Rexroth. Reprinted by permission of New Directions Publishing Corp.

Scott, Clinton, Lee. "Empty Baskets" from *Parish Parables*. Published by The Murray Press, Boston, MA. Copyright © 1946 by The Murray Press. Permission granted by the literary estate of Clinton Lee Scott.

————. "Beautiful People" from *Promise of Spring*. Published by the Unitarian Universalist Association, Boston, MA. Copyright © 1976 by the Unitarian Universalist Association. Permission granted by the literary estate of Clinton Lee Scott.